To Brian &

D0296737

1987

LOST CHILDREN
OF THE EMPIRE

LOST CHILDREN OF THE EMPIRE

**Philip Bean
and Joy Melville**

UNWIN

HYMAN

LONDON SYDNEY WELLINGTON

First published in Great Britain by the Trade Division of Unwin Hyman
Limited in 1989.

UNWIN HYMAN LIMITED
15–17 Broadwick Street, London W1V 1FP

Allen & Unwin Australia Pty Ltd
8 Napier Street, North Sydney, NSW 2060, Australia

Allen & Unwin New Zealand Pty Ltd with the Port Nicholson Press
Compusales Building, 75 Ghuznee Street, Wellington, New Zealand

---

British Library Cataloguing in Publication Data

Bean, P.
  Lost children of the Empire.
1. Great Britain. Children. Emigration to
Commonwealth countries, to 1967
I. Title   II. Melville, J.
305.213

ISBN 0–04–440358–5

Typeset in 11/12 point Sabon
by Nene Phototypesetters Ltd, Northampton
and printed at the University Press, Cambridge

To all the Child Migrants and
their families, particularly those
who have suffered in silence
for so long.

Contents

List of Illustrations

Our Gutter Children by George Cruikshank
First Canadian party
Distribution centre, Hamilton, Ontario
Dr Barnardo sees his boys off
An early group of emigrants
A party of Barnardo's girls
Barnardo boys on a farm, 1912

Arriving in Toronto
'Links of Empire welded by the Church'
'Off to Canada'
'Food all right?'
'The Work in Australia'
En route to Australia, 1932
Rhodesia House, 1950
Fairbridge boys
'A hell of a lot of independence'
Dormitories
Fairbridge boy
Royal inspection
Fairbridge girls
'Will you Help!'
Working the land
Building Bindoon
Christian Brothers Agricultural School, Bindoon, Australia
A Barnardo boy, Picton Farm, Australia
A party leaves for Australia, 1950

Acknowledgements

Thanks are due, first and foremost, to *all* the child migrants who so willingly gave up their time to talk of their experiences. These include: in Australia, Margaret Attard, Nita Brassy, John Brookman, Dorothy Chernikov, Pat Carlson, Jennifer Churchill, Francis and Violet Davis, Eileen Evett, Nigel Fitzgibbon, John Glew, Maureen Holland, Harold Jones, Edward Lewis, Alex McDonald, John McGillion, Jacqueline McKechnie, Marlene Matthews, Margaret Penry, Len Phenna, Colin Reidy, Ron Sinclair, Pamela Smedley, Maureen Trewin, Denise Trowsdale, George Wilkins, Bridget Willers; in Canada, Florence Aulph, George Barrett, Sidney Coles, Albert Crump, Charles Devonport, Phyllis Dorey, Molly Harris, Joe Jessop, George Linsdell, John McKay, William Price, G. H. Rutherford, Annie Smith, Richard Speed, Ralph Thomas, Bert Wayling; in Zimbabwe, George Brown, Susan Close, Terry French, John Gibson, Bill Hatten, Bryan Jones, Norman Mumford, Jim Neal, Reg O'Leary, Tom Paine, Ray Ponter, George Stuart, Craig Sutherland, Gilbert Walker, Francis Webster, Mike Wilkins.

Thanks, too, to those child migrants who provided information through their letters to the Child Migrants Trust, and to those who also helped, but wish to remain anonymous. Many other people provided useful information, including Maisie Wright, "Mrs Robbie" and Lyndall Eeg of Barnardo's.

Particular acknowledgement is due to Margaret Humphreys, who founded the Child Migrants Trust and who, through her work, has made a fundamental contribution to the book. David Spicer, a trustee of the Trust, has also given invaluable help. Margaret Humphreys, in turn, gratefully acknowledges the support given by the members of the Social Services Committee for Nottinghamshire County Council for the year 1987–1988.

Thanks must also be given to Domino Films who commissioned the book to accompany the television programme – in particular, to Joanna Mack for her continual support, Maggi Cook for picture research, Steve Humphries, Mary Pyke, Linda Stradling, Sue Hutton, Evelyn Denyer, Mike Fox, Fraser Barber, Nikki Clemens and Paola Ribeiro Boulting. Further thanks are due to Rod Caird, Commissioning Editor for Granada Television and

Andrew Robinson, Publishing Liaison Officer; and above all to Bill Neill-Hall and Ginny Iliff at Unwin Hyman.

Philip Bean would especially like to acknowledge Harold Jones and Edward Lewis and their families and also the assistance of John Rivers and Ros Taylor.

And final thanks to Mervyn Humphries for all his help and advice, and to Harold Frayman for releasing the book from the computer!

My Life in a Nutshell

Dorothy Chernikov has been trying to trace her family in Britain from Australia for nearly thirty years. She wrote this immediately after being told by the Child Migrants Trust that they had succeeded in doing so.

We seem to drift through life, wondering why we must put up with inferior products, inferiority complexes, and everyday problems and traumas.

Why is it that other families are well and happy? Everyone else has healthy relationships, lovely houses, win lotteries, have the best jobs. These thoughts, at times, dwell in my mind; that is until recently.

After years of working, playing, living and loving, even scraping at the bottom of the barrel to meet financial commitments, going without luxuries, with the isolated extravagance here and there, I come to the realisation that I'm a member of one of those gifted fortunate families.

I will now be able to share my thoughts and feelings with a true and caring sister or brother which will outweigh anything materially gained.

Ecstasy is my family. There is more within my family than can be found in the world.

Dorothy Chernikov
11.30 pm Saturday
10/12/88

1

An Untold Story

In 1618, a group of orphaned and destitute children left Britain for Richmond, Virginia in the United States. It was the start of an extraordinary era in British history, formally referred to as Britain's child migration scheme – a more acceptable phrase than child exportation – and was to last almost 350 years. The final boatload left only some twenty years ago, in 1967, when ninety children left Southampton for Australia, but altogether about 150,000 children were "exported" to outposts of the British Empire – to Canada, Australia, New Zealand and, to a lesser extent, South Africa, Rhodesia (now Zimbabwe) and the Caribbean.

The extraordinary part of this entire story is that the British public had, and still has, little or no idea that thousands of children were being sent out to the colonies. There was no deliberate plan or official conspiracy to keep it secret, but though there were some parliamentary debates and a number of reports and research studies have been written over the years, the scandal of what was happening was never appreciated by a really wide audience. Sometimes the very agencies that sent the children seemed, later on, to know nothing about it. One man, sent to Australia by one of the largest agencies involved in child migration, wrote to them for information on his family and got this reply from a principal social worker:

> We're sorry for the long delay in replying to your letter. I have been making enquiries on your behalf and I thought I would only write when I had something of consequence to say.
>
> I have done extensive search of our old records and I regret I can find no trace of your name anywhere. But I regret that in any event the Society did not send young children abroad, only those who wanted to emigrate, in their teens, and they went to Canada . . .
>
> I think it was unusual for young children to be sent abroad: your mother would have had to have given permission, and I wonder why you were not adopted as a baby, if she could not care for you herself? I

think you will have to rack your brains a bit more, to try to remember who cared for you as a young child . . .

From the start the child migrants were mostly aged between four and fourteen and were usually rounded up and accompanied by a Poor Law guardian or a representative from the organisation sending them. Sometimes there was no representative and the word "care" didn't come into it:

On May 20 1911, having no say in the matter, we were put on a boat and shipped to Canada. The trip was appalling, horror-laden, fraught with unconcern and disdain from those on board. We were all put in a large holding area in the ship and treated like cattle. The food was brought to the door and thrown to us. Whoever caught it, ate it.

A few of these young migrants were lucky: their existence in Britain was so bleak that they welcomed the hope of a better life in a new country. Some boys were excited about the idea of going to places like Canada, Africa and Australia. They represented adventure – cowboys and Indians and Tarzan. "I imagine my mother wasn't sending enough money to keep me," says George Barrett, who left for Canada in 1922, "and the authorities came to the school in Somerset and took me out and put me in the workhouse. And then I was in four different foster homes and the last one I was in, a little old lady and gent came in and asked me, 'Do you want to go to Canada or work under a cook?' And I said, 'Canada.' I thought of lions, tigers and bears."

Some were glad to have the chance to go, believing their prospects in Britain were slight. As Tom Paine, a child migrant to Rhodesia in 1946, says:

I was a really naughty little bugger. I would forever be standing outside the pub in Peckham [south London], asking for a packet of crisps. There would have been no future for me in war-torn Britain. I hate to think of what would have happened when my grandparents died. I would have become a thug in Peckham.

Other children eventually made a success of their new lives: they became professors, doctors, lawyers, with one "Businessman of the Year" and at least one millionaire.

But mostly the children did not want to go, they did not want to be away from familiar surroundings, and they remained permanently affected by their experience. And some of those experiences were appalling. Denise Trowsdale, sent out in 1947 at the age of eight from a Catholic Home in England to an orphanage called Nazareth House in Geraldton, Western Australia, recalls that:

The first two years were dreadful. There was this nun, she was a cruel woman – she was expelled later from the order for her cruelty, but it was too late. She had this razor strop – that's a wide leather strap for sharpening razors – and she didn't hesitate to use it, it was an everyday affair. I saw her beat four year old Cathy until she was black and blue, beaten to a pulp. I lived in fear of that woman and she played on that fear. She enjoyed it. I didn't know why I was being beaten. She would put you over her knee and hit you with a stick until you could take no more. She had the greatest influence on my life. She turned me into a scared, timid, nervy child.

In Canada, the young British children were sent to work for farmers, where they were forced into a routine which was relentlessly harsh. William Price will never forget his first job on a farm in Ontario.

I would get up at four am and go to bed at six or seven in the evening. You would work all day: you would harness the horses, clean out the stables, plough, cultivate and harrow. The farmer wouldn't feed me. I would steal stuff out of the barns, rhubarb and such, and I would go into a meal and he would cut a piece of bread in two rather than give me the whole piece. And in the mornings I would stand at the far end of the table and I would have porridge and skimmed milk while his children would have cream.

I ran away one day and this farmer came along looking for me and he pounded me at the side of the road and threw me into the front seat of the car. My Welsh temper was boiling and all I could see when I looked at him was his silly, domineering face. And I closed my fist and I hit him with it. I was very strong, though small, and the blood hit the windscreen. And he stopped the car and he knocked me out. Other children died from the cruelty.

Many child migrants, particularly those sent immediately before and after the last war, describe a deep sense of loss. They remember their childhood as dominated by a deep feeling of loneliness, whether on the Canadian prairie or in the Australian outback. Some are still bitter about being uprooted and feel rejected by both their family and country.

I never ever forgave her [mother] for the fact she signed the papers and relinquished responsibility for Sis and I. When I tracked her down in later life, I wrote her a letter of abuse and she wrote back saying we were sent out because she was poor. I just saw that as an excuse.

Nita Brassy

The whole tragedy is that so many innocent English boys with the full approval of the British government and the West Australian government, lived in a dreadful, harsh, cruel environment which I think affected many of them for the rest of their lives.   *Gordon Grant*

You would expect that transported children would be orphans or unwanted street urchins, roaming the cities in the way Dickens describes them. And child migrants were frequently *called* orphans by the agencies shipping them out because people's hearts are touched by orphans and they contribute funds for their welfare. Nevertheless, the vast majority of child migrants were *not* orphans; they were far more likely to have been abandoned, illegitimate or from a broken home. They came from all sorts of backgrounds and classes and were by no means all poor.

Their parents, when they gave their child(ren) into the care of an institution or society, generally had no idea that the children would end up being sent to the other side of the world. Some parents had offered their children for adoption but their children were shipped overseas instead, unknown to them. Some never read the small print that gave a Home the right to send the children abroad. "My mother never knew where I went to," said one man sent to Canada in 1922 when he was twelve. "She blamed my grandmother for telling the authorities she couldn't keep me any longer."

The organisations sending these children out to distant parts of the Empire were convinced that they were doing them an enormous favour. They were seen as having no prospects in Britain, of having only a remote chance of doing well and that if they remained, they would drift towards the criminal and dangerous classes. Their families were seen as failing to provide adequate care for them. Sometimes the child had been deserted and put in a Home; sometimes the strength of family ties was considered weak and unlikely to last. So what better reason could there be, the argument went, for providing care and opportunities elsewhere? Why not send these children to the colonies to start a new life, in a new unsullied environment, away from their present inhospitable world? If nothing else, their health would improve in those wide colonial spaces.

These arguments were stated so persuasively that it was clear that the children left behind would remain in a miserable, unhappy place while the children sent overseas were off to a new, shining world. The following account from *Making Rough Places Plain: fifty years' work of the Manchester and Salford boys' and girls' refuges and homes, 1870–1920*, proudly justifies sending 103 children, seventy-two boys and thirty-one girls, to Marchmont Home, in Canada:

> Let us give the particular case of one of the boys. He was twelve years of age when admitted, neglected and living amid demoralising surroundings almost unmentionable, his mother was in prison for repeated acts of an abominable character, his father was unknown, the lad likely never had known him. After coming out of prison the mother signed our form giving us charge of the lad and tramped off to some Yorkshire town. Now think of the prospect before this bright English boy. It all pointed to abject poverty and degradation, if not to crime.
>
> To put himself out of reach of this evil influence he chose to go to Canada and now within twelve months we have a letter from him, and it would perhaps be difficult to find a lad in happier and healthier surroundings. The contrast in the actual condition and prospects of the lad within about twelve months is more like a fairy transformation than reality, the gain – costing in cash about £11 – is inestimable. To a girl the benefit is often even greater in being thus removed from demoralising conditions. Again, multiply this by 103 and put down the answer in moral and material gain to the lad and to Empire.

Unfortunately, when you look more closely at the reasons for child migration, less high-minded and rather more pragmatic motives appear. The public face of the scheme may have been directed towards the welfare of the child but no one could deny there were advantages to the agencies sending them. In the late nineteenth century, for instance, it cost about £12 a year to look after a child in an institution in Britain. To send one overseas was a one-off payment of £15. Sometimes the "welfare" of the parents was the main object. The scheme became such a useful way of disposing of an unwanted child that one organisation refused to take any more illegitimate children, in case illegitimacy was seen to be encouraged.

Children in local authority care had to have the approval of the Secretary of State before being sent overseas. But this approval was not needed for children in the care of voluntary organisations like Barnardo's, the Fairbridge Society, the Church of England Advisory Council on Empire Settlement, the Church of England Children's Society, the Catholic Council for British Overseas Settlements and so on. Once a child was placed with an organisation, it was responsible for them until they reached the age of majority. Each made arrangements for the child migrants on arrival but there was no standard way of dealing with them. Sometimes they went to individual, isolated farmhouses to work; sometimes they remained in orphanages, children's Homes or farm schools; sometimes they went to live in families as foster children.

The whole movement consisted of a number of different schemes run by different voluntary agencies or philanthropists: the only common thread was the shared aim of transporting "good British stock" from Britain throughout the Empire. Preserving the Empire was regarded as all-important and its need for British children to keep the flag flying was piously equated with the children's need for its vast spaces. The Catholic agencies summed up this attitude in 1938:

> Those who are co-operating with His Eminence [Cardinal Hinsley] and the other bishops of England in this great and noble project of transplanting poor children who are without means, influence, and parentless in many cases, from congested and unpromising surroundings, to a land rich in natural, but undeveloped resources which are awaiting the correct type of people to render them productive, are doing much to strengthen and extend the Empire, to preserve and augment our Christian civilisation which is so seriously threatened at the present time, and to give poor boys similar opportunities to advance in life to those open to the sons of comfortably-circumstanced parents.

But the reality was a bit different. As one boy who was sent to a Catholic orphanage in Australia said, "They didn't give us much schooling. I am very, very bitter about that. We would go to school at nine o'clock and we'd be out of school by ten o'clock and out working."

Voluntary organisations and successive governments shared the absolute certainty that what they were doing was right and you can only marvel at the tenacity, self-righteousness and insensitivity of those involved. Despite criticism, which as early as 1877, described child migration as "inhuman" and exposing children "to great disadvantages and to much obloquy", youngsters continued to be transported overseas. Other critics spoke of the "total absence of efficient supervision, which exposed the children to suffering and wrong, for which they found neither relief nor redress". But still the children went.

It was not that the administration at the British end was poor: far from it. On arrival overseas, the children were sent off to distribution centres or direct to farms, farm schools or orphanages. But those responsible for sending the children out were often ignorant of the conditions to which they were sending them. Young children arrived dressed in blazers, short trousers or skirts in the middle of a Canadian winter. Charles Devonport remembers arriving at Halifax harbour in 1922.

> After 24 hours or so we unloaded there, and us twelve boys were ushered into the Department of Immigration shed, which was very

cold and draughty: the wind blew in one end and out the other, and we were seated on dirty benches along the edges of the building – a massive, cold concrete-type building. And after a bit a chap came and told us to get on board this train, a small train which was only going a matter of thirty miles to a small town in Nova Scotia called Windsor.

We arrived at the Windsor railway station approximately nine o'clock at night, and we waited in the waiting room for a while, and eventually two teams of horses came and we were loaded on them. As soon as we got outside we realised how bitterly cold it was, so we all huddled together, because we had no suitable winter clothing – there were no extra robes or anything like that. So we went three miles in the bitter cold and the rain and the sleet. They hadn't thought to bring extra covering to put over us, to make the ride more comfortable. There was no consideration given to the boys' comfort right from the word go. No, none at all.

Young girls arrived on farms on the prairies or Ontario farmlands to work as servant girls, knowing nothing of the country, the families to whom they were going or the kind of work they were expected to do. Although it was the boys who were meant to help on the farm, while the girls did domestic work, in reality the girls had to do whatever they were told to. As Annie Smith, who left Middlemore Homes, in Birmingham, for Canada in 1928, says:

When you are young and go out to another country, the country is strange, the people are strange, the customs are different and you don't know what to expect; it's all new and you don't know what to make of it. You are at a disadvantage. And so many times you think, "I have just got to make the best of it. I'm here and can't go back." Home was across the Atlantic Ocean.

Once on the farm, Annie says she did the housework and "everything there was to do on the farm. I think the only thing I never learned to do was milk the cows. I planted, picked, hoed corn and all the veg, picked bugs off the potatoes."

Young British boys, sent off to Australian orphanages at seven, eight or nine, were then sent off a few years later to work on farms. They had no knowledge of farming and no interest in finding out so it was hardly surprising that they were considered poor at their job; or to hear that they were often abused, both physically and mentally.

With the best will in the world it would have been practically impossible to check on all the children once they were on their isolated farms, given the vast distances involved in Canada or Australia. Inspectors from the distribution Homes visited farms in

Canada, sometimes annually, but it was very easy for the farmers to cover-up matters if they wished. As George Barrett recalls:

> When Mr Ray [supervisor of the Halifax distribution centre] came to see how I was, the old chap would say I was out in the fields. He wouldn't let me contact Mr Ray and he would say, "George is making out fine." I should have run away, but I was really afraid.

This visit as least represents an attempt to find out how the children were doing but there is no excuse for the continued ignorance, especially at the British end, of the appalling abuse that so often took place. No one checked what was happening to British children in the Australian institutions (see Nigel Fitzgibbon's experiences in the next chapter). Nor is there any excuse for the way many organisations deliberately told children their parents were dead or that they had no family, when this was a lie. Most organisations believed it was better to cut off the child from its previous "deprived" life but the scars remain into adulthood – particularly the desperation to find any kind of family.

Many of these child migrants, now adults, cannot speak of their experiences without tears. It is time their voices are heard.

2

"You weren't supposed to have feelings"

What was it actually like to be a child migrant? To be shipped overseas to a country you knew nothing about, for reasons you did not understand. To be faced, after the mild climate of Britain, with Canadian temperatures sometimes forty degrees below zero, when you could lose an ear through frostbite, or with the pulverising heat of Australia, where temperatures reach 110 degrees or more. To find yourself in an isolated Canadian farmhouse, sometimes working sixteen hours a day out in the fields, or in a Home in Australia that you have to help build yourself with rocks from the bush.

What was it like to find that it's merely the luck of the draw whether you end up with caring foster parents or being cruelly and systematically abused? To discover that because you have come from a Home in Britain you are regarded as trash. To realise that because the policy of the organisation sending you overseas is to withhold your records from you, you will not even be aware that your mother or father is still alive, that you have a sister or brother living in another country or that there is a disease in your family which, unknowingly, you may pass on to your children. To be unaware that your name or birthday has been carelessly changed or that you can't get a passport because you haven't enough family information. To be ignorant of the fact that you have missed out on your legal rights, that you have not only failed to inherit any money, however little the sum, but also any trinkets or family photographs that every "normal" person treasures as proof of identification with their family.

What became of these children when they became adults? How did they cope and survive? The life stories of the following five child migrants, still living in the countries they were originally sent to, give a clear picture of the trauma they went through and the lasting effect on their adult lives.

FLORENCE AULPH is now eighty-seven years old. Born into a family of seven children, in a small village near Newcastle, she came out to Canada in 1913 when she was twelve and a half.

> We were so very poor. My father was slowly dying of TB from working in the coal mines. I was not able to get around like the rest of the family, as I sort of dragged one of my legs. I used to sit in my little rocking chair beside my Daddy and we kept each other company. In the meantime Mother was expecting another baby.
> One day Mother picked me up and said she was taking me to a place called Babies' Castle, a Dr Barnardo's Home for crippled children. She said they would straighten out my leg and then she would come and get me. I will never forget that place, I clung to my mother. But it was all prearranged. I was simply devastated. I never saw my mother again. One day a nurse came in and told me I had no daddy, he had gone to heaven. So I would have to stay with them.

With no consultation, Florence was told she would be going to Canada.

> We went down to the docks in carriages drawn by four horses, where the big ship was waiting. We were three weeks crossing and most of us were dreadfully seasick all the way.
> There was one incident that happened while we were on board the ship which had a real sobering effect on all of us. We were crossing the Atlantic Ocean and we got playing around on the deck there and the waves were getting pretty rough and beating on the iron railings. A sailor put up a rope and warned us, "Don't none of you go under that as a wave might come up and dash you against the railings." Well, the girls didn't try it. But some of the boys sort of made a game of it. They would dodge under the rope and when the waves rose up over the railings they would run back under the rope.
> One little guy, a skinny little urchin, ran there and ran back, but a bigger wave came along and caught him and we were stunned. I will never forget it, it pushed him against the railings and killed him. And the sailors made a plain coffin and they tried to explain that no way could they keep him on board as the whales could smell something dead for miles and they would come in and turn the boat upside down and we would all be drowned. And so it was best that we have a little funeral service for him. They put a box on top of the railings and put a Union Jack over it. We stood there speechless: we couldn't believe he was going to be thrown overboard. I cried and cried.
> Someone was looking after us, but take 200 children, you can't watch them all. Two or three adults would walk around and tell us, "Don't do this" and we were so used to hearing that. But the funeral really sobered us.
> We landed at Quebec and we then had to go on a small boat down the St Lawrence River and it was kind of nice, and then we went to Peterborough and it was a children's Home, a great big building. There

were a hundred boys and a hundred girls, but there was another place for the boys in another building.

They had our names all down in a book and they would take a couple of us in the room at a time and ask us, "Where would you like to live, in the city or out on a farm?" And stupid me said, "On a farm." I did everything the hard way.

And that was the way we were sorted out. And the first place I went to was Hagersville. It was called a foster home, just me and two little boys, and they were good to me. I went to school while there for just one year, as I did so want to pass my Entrance into high school. And that's as far as I got. There was not as much stress put on education as there is today. I never went off the place, only to school. I never played with the other kids, we were just Home kids and you just weren't supposed to have any feelings. You weren't considered as good as the rest of the kids, because you had no home of your own and no parents.

You don't know what this does to you. I have never got over it; even now when I meet someone who is a bit hoity-toity, I cringe and yet I have nothing to be ashamed of. I got terribly withdrawn as it seemed nobody wanted me, only for the work I did.

As a Home child, you have no say in anything. You are still under their thumb. I worked for my board after school and Saturdays and Sundays. I worked, but I loved to work. I split wood and carried it in a huge box they put in the kitchen. There was no water in the house, no bathroom, and there wasn't a toy in the place. I did housework and looked after the two kiddies and they tried to adopt me and they wrote to my mother and she said, "No way, you took her to Canada, but you still don't own her." But what was the difference? I never saw her again. I used to feel so bitter about it, but when I got older I realised the circumstances. It must have been just as hard on her as it was on me.

I was at Hagersville for three years. Then suddenly one day I was picked up, no reason, and sent to Fergus. It was a dreadful place. I had a life of hell there. The man had a vicious temper and he used to beat me up if I forgot something or didn't do it right. I was just a bundle of nerves. You see, I was the hired man and a housemaid too. I worked my heart and soul out there for $3 per month, $36 per year. It kept me with something to wear on my feet, that's all, and people threw some of their old clothes at me and I would sit up till midnight, putting a pin here and a pin there; and that's how I learned to sew. I had no money, I couldn't do anything else.

I came out with another girl from England, Maud, but she chose a city life. She wrote me a letter one time and said she would dearly love to come and see me if the people would allow it and I was scared skinny and I handed them the letter and the women said, "Well why not, just come Saturday." So she came and we were washing dishes and he [the farmer] came storming into the house and said, "I want you out at the barn, right now." Well, he beat me up but good, bashed me round the head. I was nothing but a nervous wreck. It seemed I had forgotten to grind up the turnips that morning for the young cattle.

Maud and I went up to our bedroom. I was still crying, and she said, "What went on out there? I want to know." And I said, "Nothing more than usual. If I forget something or don't do something I am supposed to, I get a good cuffing." And she couldn't believe her ears and said, "I am going to get you out of here," and I said, "I am tied."

I was eighteen and legally I was free to go anywhere I wanted. But I did not know more than a kid of twelve, I had been kept shut in for so long. I was just plain dumb and stupid. Maud wrote and said "There's a lady living two doors down from me in Sarnia who wants a maid real bad and you'd get $1 a day and every Wednesday afternoon off and every other Sunday, so we could both go to a movie." And I had never seen a movie in my life.

I had a little tin trunk with my worldly belongings in it and I thought, "How am I going to get that out?" So finally I handed her [the farmer's wife] Maud's letter and she was furious, she thought she had me for life, cheap labour. She kept the letter until her husband came in and she handed it to him and they were really shook up, they thought they had a good thing going.

They consented to take me to the train. And the lady sent me the price of my ticket. I had no money. That was the big problem: what can you do with $3 a month? When she came to meet me from the train she stood and looked at me and started to laugh and it upset me. Of course, I did not realise what I looked like, so old-fashioned. She said, "Never mind my dear girl, we will go shopping for clothes next Wednesday" and I had never been in a store. I was never so happy, working for this lady. I had never learned any fancy baking, but I soon did.

I was twenty-two when I got married. I met him in Sarnia and we got along famous. I had been through the mill and was beat up, so a word of kindness went a long way. We married in the Depression years and it was pretty rough going. We moved into a little log cabin with dirt floors and not a cupboard anywhere. I took newspapers and scalloped them all at the edges. And I would go out and split wood and dry it in the oven and it would start with a match. We couldn't afford to buy newspapers to start a fire.

There was no drainage and one year the fields were under water and the soil turned sour. We worked our heart and soul out, but there was nothing there to work on. We rented for a while, then found a nice little home. It did need fixing up, but I worked like a slave. My husband was a farmer. We raised 500 chickens every year and I cleaned eggs every day, washed them and packed them and the lorry came every week. We were there for nineteen years and I raised three children and until my husband died and I had a fall and had to come to this Home, I was as happy as a lark. But nobody has any idea what we Home children went through.

My mother did not have too much education, and couldn't write. I kept in contact with the family until my mother died. I just have one sister left and she came over, she said she had to see me once. But we were not sisters, we were strangers, there was no feeling of family, kinship, there couldn't be.

Florence now lives in an old people's Home in Ontario where many of the inmates are senile or disabled, though she herself is bright and alert.

I started life out in a little orphan Home at four and I end up here in another Home, and sometimes I wonder if there is a God. I went through so much when I was a youngster and to think I have to end up in a Home again. There's no one to get me out, it just doesn't seem fair. But I guess the good Lord is not through with me yet.

CHARLES DEVONPORT also went to Canada as a child. His main trauma concerns his mother. She was alive when he went to Canada but when he asked about her in later years, he was told she was dead and accepted this without checking, unaware that there was such a thing as a death certificate. As he grew older, his resolve to find out something about his mother – even just the location of her grave – strengthened. What shocked him was that he found, eventually, that she had been alive long after he was told she was dead. He has now visited her grave in England twice, deeply upset at having found he missed her by only a few years.

His memories of his childhood in Nottingham and, above all, his first months in Canada are still only too clear. He remembers being in a Nottingham workhouse for about a year because of "lung sickness, bronchitis, and an intestinal problem due to malnutrition".

Then the Child Welfare Society took me away from my mother who couldn't look after me and work as well, and put me in a foster home.

Just outside Nottingham there were orchards, but they were surrounded by iron railings. And we would gaze at the lovely apples. One evening we jacked the railings apart and got in and this big chap with leather leggings on and two dogs caught us. Then this huge bobby came on his bicycle and I wound up in front of the magistrate. I was sentenced to one year probation and had to go to a branch of the Nottingham's Boys' Brigade for two days a week for a year in lieu of going to reform school.

At the club, twelve boys were asked to volunteer to go to Canada, to the Dakeyne Boys' Farm. Although forty applied, Charles Devonport was one of those chosen.

Two weeks later we were given instructions to pack our clothing and be on the railway platform of the London and Midland Railway. And I was sitting there on my little suitcase and I heard footsteps and my mother was walking along the platform towards me – she spotted me right away. And I was sitting there with my head in hands and she said, "Teddy, you're leaving me." I said, "Yes mother, I'm going to Canada." So she says, "I've brought you something" and I stood up of course and my mother gave me a five pound note and a box camera. And she told me to save my money and be a good boy and write to her, and then she kissed me again and started to cry. And she wrote me one letter. I answered that letter faithfully and I wrote another letter later on to the same address. She replied once and after that there were no more letters, ever.

We finally boarded the ship and after ten days we arrived in Halifax and us twelve boys were loaded on this small train going to a small town in Nova Scotia called Windsor. We arrived at Windsor and as the weather was bad we went into the only door we could see, which was into a dirty shed. And we waited there approximately one hour until finally it was getting dark. Eventually two teams of horses came pulling sleds on runners. And no one said a word, it was all grim silence and it was three miles from the Windsor railway station to the farm and we were all huddled together in these vehicles. We pulled up to the farmhouse back door and I went to jump out, but the chappie, he said, "Just a minute. We've got to go to the barn and do some work before the turkey supper."

I objected because we were cold and wet and no one paid attention. They drove us up to the barn which was a considerable distance away and we went in and they handed us forks and shovels and took us down some steps to where the cattle were – it was warm down there, that was one good thing – and told us to get to work.

We looked at each other, work at what? And they explained we had to move that manure which the cattle was standing in, had been all day, to a manure carrier. And we had to lift the manure up and put it in there until it was really full, and then the boys would push it outdoors and dump it. Nobody had the commonsense to show us how to dump it, so there was a lot more time lost, figuring it out. I was starving and I spied this pail and I looked round rather furtively and nobody was watching me and it was full of milk. I blew the dust away and I put my nose in it and I got myself a good tummy-full of milk and I felt much better then.

After a short time they decided that we weren't going to be able to clean that barn out before morning, so they told us to go up to the house and get something to eat. So we went sloshing through the rain. I had shoes on and was ill-prepared for this sort of weather. We arrived at the farmhouse and the woman came and told us in a rather rough voice to wash ourselves and then go into the alleged dining room where there was a meal laid out for us on these long rough tables. The meal consisted of corn bread and molasses and lukewarm hashed potatoes and pitchers of skimmed milk.

We were tired and hungry, so I ate something and the rest of the boys followed suit, and then she showed us where we were to sleep. It was up the stairs in a long room over the dining room – it's still there to this day – and we were told to choose our own beds. Well, they were very scantily covered: at the most there was two or three thin blankets, one thin pillow, and that was it. And there was no heating in the dormitory at all: it was miserable. The only way I could keep warm was to lay on the mattress and get under all three blankets and keep my clothes on. Although they had dried out in the barn to some extent, they were still damp and dirty.

No one came up to see that we were comfortable – no one! We were just ordered up there like a bunch of cattle or slaves or whatever, and left to our own devices. Having had a rough day, we finally dozed off and none of the boys spoke to each other, not one, and I saw this rope at the foot of my bed and as I was dozing off I wondered what it was. At five o'clock the next morning I found out. I heard this awful, deafening clanging noise and I woke up, and I saw the rope going up and down and then it dawned on me: there was a bell up there to wake us all up. They also used it to call us in from the fields for the midday meal.

It was still snowing and raining and the chap who looked after the farm, he came up the stairs and gave us some sarcastic talk about being lain in bed all day. So we all got back into our clothes, which were still rather damp and went downstairs after him and he handed each one of us a milk pail. We all trooped down to the barn in the slosh and he set each one of us down by a cow and told us to milk it. He didn't come to us and explain the principle of milking. He showed no concern for our condition, our physical condition. He just sat there and watched us struggling to get the milk out of the cow. Of course, we caught on after a bit.

And then after the milk was gathered in they took us up to the house for breakfast. It was roughly the same food that we'd had the night previously, but the potato hash was a little warmer and there was some tea instead of skimmed milk. And he stood there and as soon as we'd finished, probably fifteen minutes later, he would order us outside and we would follow the hired man to the orchard. It was our job, regardless of the weather, to gather up the boughs and load them on the carts. There was still snow in the woods in June and it was cold for us, because we had no winter clothing.

We'd work till there was no more daylight. Then we would come in, in the evening, late evening, and milk the cows again. By then I'd be so tired that I'd literally collapse on my bed with no thought of going anywhere at all. And of course the days were getting longer. That meant we would be out working longer.

Then they moved us to other jobs, getting the hay out, cutting the silo so it could be fed to the cows. It was all hard work because we were not big children, we were small for our age. Nobody seemed to care much about our welfare, there was no human kindness devoted to us, we were never spoken to in a mannerly way, always looked upon rather contemptuously. Maybe it was because we were boys from the reform school era. They didn't care one jot whether we lived or died really, as long as we did the work. We was just considered as little slavies, there temporarily until we could be got rid of, to make room for another bunch of slavies, young children, coming out from England.

The fellow that operated the place, he never spoke to us or gave us a word of advice. He just treated us like we were mere numbers. If he saw an opportunity to deprive us of a few dollars, why, he would do so. The women in Windsor, for example, used to gather used clothing and bring it out to the farms to give to the boys, free. But this chap, if he thought you had a few dollars, he would charge you for whatever clothing *he* thought you needed.

One by one the boys went – either decided to pack it in and go elsewhere, or someone would come from a local farm and hire them, which is what happened to me eventually.

JOE JESSOP was one of the second wave of children who went out to the Fairbridge Farm School at Duncan, Vancouver Island in Canada, between 1935 and 1948. No isolated farm house for him, instead an isolated farm school. His experiences differ from those of the earlier children but there is the same bewilderment and bitterness about being shipped 6,000 miles away from his English Home, trying to adapt to a totally different way of life and a lack of access to records so that, much later, he discovered that even his birthday was not the date he was told. Born in 1930, he was sent out to Canada in 1937.

I was at Middlemore Homes in Birmingham and the next thing I knew I was on a boat to Canada. We were just like cattle. When you are seven you don't really comprehend what is going on.

I would say there were twenty in my group. We were on the *Duchess of Atholl* and we ended up in Halifax. The first thing was we were all lined up in front of the train to have our picture taken: it was put on the wall of the office at Fairbridge Farm School. After a train journey of three or four days, and a long ferry ride, I remember getting on a big bus which took us to the school. And the kids were around the big gates there, waving and cheering, there seemed hundreds there already. I guess I took it as an adventure more than anything else, but my most startling experience was all those little kids yelling. I remember thinking, *where* am I?

We were segregated, the girls at one end of the school and the boys at the other; and until we were twelve we wore short blue pants and horrible sweaters. We were delegated to another group of about twenty-five and that group stayed together in a cottage under the care of a cottage mother.

You would get up in the morning and go to this gigantic dining room and have your breakfast. Then you went to school. It was a whole self-contained community: the school was there, the farm was there. We ate what we grew. We were well fed. I can remember porridge on the table and peanut butter and jam on toast, but you couldn't have both. You came back to the dining room for lunch, then back to school. And then after school, at 3 pm, you worked on the farm for about two hours, picking potatoes and so on.

There was no time to ourselves. After farming work, there was the cottage mother to contend with and what she wanted us to do. The seniors picked on us worse than anybody else. And they used to make us fight each other. And there was a guy who was strong and they would pretend to let him beat me, and he would have a re-match and beat the hell out of me. There was bullying from the old kids to the new kids. In the bathroom they had a hole in the door and if you were having a bath and one of the seniors asked you to stand up, if you had an erection you were in trouble.

The cottages were like an army H-hut, separated in the middle. This would be classified as two cottages. It was really kind of nice. There were twenty-five to a dormitory and a dining room in each cottage and the cottage mother's bedroom and sitting room were upstairs. Downstairs there was a big play area and laundry tubs for washing our tin plates and cups. There was a lot of clanging when washing them in these tubs, just like a prison. And there was a big long trough where you had the taps coming out for washing your face. There were four toilets and a bath.

We did not have to go out of the farm school at all, except once a year you would go to the movies, when you had raised enough allowance, fifty cents. We got one cent a week for pocket money until thirteen, then a nickel a week.

There was always total authority around you at all times. One time, they said everyone had to have their tonsils out and the whole school was sent off. The cottage mother was a strict disciplinarian. She would beat you if you did something wrong. It was a way of life. I had to rake the yard one day and I did not finish it, maybe I was slow, and that was enough to get the strap in the morning. If you were not liked by your cottage mother, your life was hell, really. She had complete control over us, she did not have to answer to anybody, she was our keeper. She had total dominance. I think I just got a bad one. There were some nice ones.

I remember one time when the cottage mother and some other woman got me in their sitting room and decided to strip me. I was about ten or eleven. And as far as I know nothing happened. I was fighting, but whether they gave up, or what, it was humiliating. But who can you turn to? You don't even tell the rest of the kids.

I was embittered at that time: the main question was, why am I here? However, you were too busy with survival. You had no money. The bitterness died because you did not let it ruin your life. When you got out on your own, you saw family life which we had never had in all our life. At Christmas there was never any surprise, because they had a catalogue and you had to pick your gift out prior to Christmas. You could have one up to three dollars. And I was nine and was trying to tell these other kids that there wasn't a Santa Claus and the cottage mother heard me and when I got down on Christmas morning, I got a piece of coal and that was it. And all the other kids got oranges and nuts. And I cried that day; but I started believing in Santa.

There was no *love*. There were times after I was about twelve that you might get a girl to go down to the river with you, but you did not know what the hell to do and sat there and held hands.

There were good times there, too. We played baseball or softball. The way you learned to swim, they had a river with this great big log and you walked or were dragged up this log and you jumped off it and swam to the raft. There were a couple of them drowned in this river. And I remember we used to have to go to church on Wednesdays to learn the hymns we were going to have on Sunday. The priest was another mean guy. If you did not sound right he would keep you there until you did. We could stay there until nine at night.

Me and another guy, I guess we were in everybody's bad books because we were continually getting the strap. Maybe I was a hellion. I really did not have a childhood. If you were good academically, you continued your education. I know I was just average. But very few of us went further educationally. It was in their power: they would pick who they wanted to.

At fifteen, they got you your first job: you generally worked on a farm in the neighbourhood. I worked on a chicken farm and then went to different farms for a while. I got $25 a month, $12.50 of which went back to the school until you were eighteen. They saved it for you and I got some. Then I went to the big city, Vancouver, scared out of my tree, and joined the CPR [Canadian Pacific Railway] and was there two years. Then I joined the army. In between leaving the CPR and joining the army, I rode the box cars and lived in the seediest part of Vancouver. Usually when you're down and out, you have a family to go to. Well, I wasn't going back to the school. Yet Fairbridge was my home. I joined the army for survival and stayed there six years.

My birth certificate, the short version, just arrived in an envelope on my twenty-first birthday almost to the day. I was always told my birthday was June 24 and then I found it was June 7. And at twenty-one years I had to change over to thinking I was younger. Fairbridge must have had some records, but we were not privy to them at all. It was a closely guarded secret.

NIGEL FITZGIBBON was one of 10,000 or so children who were shipped to Australia after the Second World War. The systematic abuse of some of the children in the Australian institutions to which these children were sent is one of the blackest spots in the whole history of child migration. During the early days of child migration, attitudes to children were as cruel and intolerant in Britain as they were overseas. But what happened to many children in Australia in the 1940s and 1950s, a time when we were meant to be so much more aware of child welfare, was horrific.

On 15 August 1947, Nigel boarded the SS *Astaurius* with about 250 other boys and girls destined for orphanages in Australia. Both his parents were in fact alive, even if they hadn't been contacted for permission for their son to go to Australia. His mother was a Catholic and his father a Protestant and before Nigel was left at a Catholic Home, under his mother's maiden name, his mother had to fulfil the Home's condition that he be baptised a Catholic. His sister went into a Catholic Home for girls: it was standard procedure to separate brothers and sisters. The two only met in adulthood. It was, he remembers, good fun on board, with lots of games and activities. After some six weeks, the boat docked at Fremantle.

> There was a band on the wharf to meet us and the Archbishop came down and we all had to prostrate ourselves, we were all blessed. It was a beautiful September day. I'd never seen budgerigars in my life and they had cages and cages of these beautiful birds. We got on this bus and some of my friends went on the back of another truck. I never saw them again.

The other children were being taken off to different orphanages, often hundreds of miles apart. Nigel, in a group of twenty, went to Bindoon Boys' Town, a Catholic orphanage, isolated in the bush about sixty miles north of Perth. They were the first batch of post-war children to go there and Nigel was impressed with the green hills and grapevines on the side of the road. But on arrival at the orphanage, there was little chance to admire the view.

> After we'd had our new clothes taken off us, we were given some khaki clothes and next day we started fitting into the routine. Being on a farm, there was cows to milk first thing in the morning and that sort of thing. There was no real education, because they had no qualified school teachers there and we didn't care. There were only four or five Brothers there at the time and the Brother in charge was a good man. But a few months later, Brother McGee left and then we got told about this man, Brother Keaney, coming back. And he arrived. And what he'd done was, he started pulling the boys out of the classrooms, 'cos he wanted to start building projects: massive building projects.

Within three years they built three large two storey buildings with spacious hallways and chapels, dormitories and school rooms. Each building was made of stone and granite that the boys brought from the bush and cemented in place. As well as the main college buildings, the boys built dams for the farm, digging out the earth by hand with pick and shovel, numerous farm buildings and various Roman Catholic monuments.

It was sheer slave labour with primitive tools from dawn till late evening. It was so *cruel*. We had cement burns on our hands and feet and our bodies were emaciated from the inadequate diet: we had gruel for breakfast which was mixed with bran from the chicken feed. There was no regard whatsoever to safety. We'd be right up on the scaffolding which we'd made ourselves out of trees we'd cut down, carrying enormous weights. One day when I was building, I had my head split open with a falling bucket with concrete in it.

But it wasn't just inanimate objects that injured the boys. Only three days after Brother Keaney arrived, Nigel encountered his brutality.

He said, "Gibby, come here," and I went up to this man, I was only a little, skinny rump of a kid, and I said, "Yes Brother." He said, "What do you want to be when you grow up?" and I just looked at this man and said, "I don't know, Brother" and without warning, this huge fist the size of a saucepan came out and smacked into my face and I went sprawling. I must have done a couple of somersaults across the concrete floor.

I wasn't knocked out, but my nose was bleeding and I sat up and I could see this huge man calling me to come back to him. So I got up and as I approached him again he said, "Come closer." And I looked up into his eyes and he was looking round, to make sure nobody else was around the place. And I could feel the blood trickling down from my broken nose into my mouth.

He said to me once more, "What do you want to be when you grow up?" and I could see this arm coming again and I thought, I've got to say something here. I always like chucks, chickens, ducks in England because we had a poultry farm close to us. And straight away I blurted out, "A poultry farmer, Brother." And he just said, "Right. Get the heck out of here and get down with the chucks."

And I went running out and as I was going to grab the door to open it, the next thing I felt this huge heavy cosh, a heavy strap with metal in it, hit me behind my head and split my head open. And I went running off and I cried for a while, here I was, thirteen years of age, and I'd met this huge man and been assaulted by him. I can never forget it, *never*. You just couldn't work out why it had come to you, or if you deserved it, or what had happened. There was no one there to protect you.

I felt like running away, but where could I go to? There was a priest there, a Benedictine monk, who I knew was homosexual, and I had reservations about going to him. My last thoughts that night, before I went to bed, were "Where's my father?" For a thirteen year old kid it was traumatic.

I think it was an act of humiliation, which was a very common thing with this huge Christian Brother for any simple act of misdoing, like if you left the bags of cement out in the weather and they got wet. A formal type of punishment you would get from him is that you'd be made to stand up on a table that high, and in front of the other boys –

remember we had boys aged from ten to sixteen – you'd be made to drop your trousers in full view of them. And his favourite expression was, "Lift up your curtain, Biddy Ann." He always called you by girls' names. An Irish girl's name.

And then you'd be thrashed by a heavy strap, sometimes with a reinforced stretch of electric wiring in it. Some of the Brothers made up straps themselves. They were very good at it. They had four strands of heavy leather and had metal plates in there, or rows of pennies between the layers of straps to give it weight and flexibility. It was part and pattern of the whole way of life.

Nigel said that a number of the other Brothers sexually abused the boys.

This bloke, on four or five occasions, he did it to me. He'd feel your crutch area and use one ruse or another, like that it was a medical for worm infections, to fully explore your anal region.

But what really seems to have really broken Nigel's spirit and left a life-long scar, is the sheer physical brutality and sadism of Brother Keaney.

Keaney had a special stick which had – and I'm an ex-army man – a bullet on the end of it. Now if you know a 303 bullet, the bullet goes inside a casing like a shell, but the shell casing has got rivets on it. And what he'd do with this stick after he'd hit you, he'd give you a quick thrust up the rectum and give it a twist and that would withdraw your lower bowel out of your rectum and that happened to me once. He must have thought he hurt me pretty badly, because he inspected me some time after that.

The same Brother did this to another boy. A few hours after, Nigel said to him:

"You're weeping from your bum, you'll have to have some treatment, some medical treatment. Look, do you feel anything?" And he said, "I've got something between my legs." And I lifted his pants and I saw this pink tissue, the lower part of his rectum, hanging out. And I said, "There's a box that's got ointments in and things down at the dairy." Cows often had what I call collapsed udders or something and so I had seen where they sort of put it back in . . . and I got a screwdriver, the blunt end of it, and I made cotton wool pads which I lubricated a bit, and then I slowly and eventually got the intestine, the lower bowel, back into his rectum. And I said, "You mustn't go to the toilet, because I think it'll come out again."

You *can't* forget those things. And I think it made a lot of kids there very hardened.

Nigel left Bindoon when he was seventeen and a half and, despite his experiences, gives the impression of having made a go of life. He joined the army and was there for twenty-two years, becoming a Warrant Officer, Class 1, and winning lots of medals. His discharge papers are full of praise for his service and character. He married and had children, though his marriage was not a great success. He is now separated from his wife, which he mostly attributes to his life at Bindoon.

A lot of those kids never married and if they did have a relationship with a woman, a normal relationship with a woman, it often didn't last because you never felt the tenderness, the feel of a close relationship with anyone, in your young life. You saw violence, day after day.

Nigel now lives in Perth and works for a timber merchant. He didn't try to find his mother or father or sister when younger and it was his sister, who stayed in Wales, who found him in the 1950s, but they have never become close. Nigel eventually went back to Britain and discovered that his father had died the year before, and he now regrets that he didn't try to find his family earlier. He is deeply affected by his experiences, "I look back and think my misfortunes in life are partly because of my upbringing there."

PAMELA SMEDLEY went into a Catholic orphanage in London shortly after her birth. At eighteen months she was sent to another one in Middlesbrough, where she stayed until she was twelve. Then one of the nuns asked which girls wanted to go to Australia and, thinking it sounded like a nice day trip, Pamela put up her hand.

And then we come out here and, bang, we came to *another* orphanage. I couldn't believe it. We sat on the iron steps at Goodwood and cried; we sat there and cried for three days. And it was so hot, up in the hundreds. We just wanted to get on a ship and come home to England. Talk about from the fat into the fire. I had this feeling of loss and senselessness. I thought how am I ever going to see England again, how am I going to find anybody all the way out here, what chance did I have of seeing my best friend in England? I felt so alone.

The Reverend mother was very, very strict and very, very cruel . . . she used to belt us for what we thought were trivial things. At the end of one prayer we were supposed to say, "God bless Australia", and no way were we going to bless Australia, we hated Australia when we first come out here. And all the English girls in unison sang out "God bless England." We all got put across the bed and thrashed for that, she really belted us with the leather strap, the ones they wore round their waists. The strap was that wide, and they had their rosary beads, big long wooden rosary beads, hanging on the end of it. Of course we really hated Australia even more after that.

Pamela was fifteen when she was sent out to a shearing station some five hours' drive from Adelaide, in parched dry countryside where temperatures in the summer rose to well over one hundred degrees. It was an isolated farm, miles from anywhere.

To me, it was Mars! It was so different from the English countryside: it was flat and dry and the trees were great big ugly gum trees. I still don't like gum trees. I was getting sent away again, you know, even further away. Talk about being punished for something you didn't do.

I hated it. I cried myself to sleep every night. I was cut off from all the friends I ever had. Here's me, a slip of a kid, cooking for seven shearers. I had to cook morning tea for them, cook lunch, cook tea. They used to call their dinner tea. I worked like a navvy – I *hated* it. I had to get up at dawn, and they had a big, a very old-fashioned place with wooden floors and a great big huge wooden table. And you'd have to light the stove of a morning to heat the water. And they had seven children I had to wash for and clean for.

It was a very hard life on the farm, such a cruel life, so lonely. I was always the servant, always made to feel like, "You're lucky you've got this job. We took you out and we're looking after you." I got one weekend off in six and the rest of the time I was working.

The woman that I worked for, she'd sit down and fan herself and make out she was having a heart attack, so that I used to get so frightened that she was going to drop dead on me. I used to work twice as hard, so she wouldn't die. Because I thought, if she died, I'd get the blame for it. I was that used to getting the blame for things that I didn't do at the convent, it wasn't going to be any different now I was out.

I was paid £1.2s.6d. a week and I had to buy clothes and everything out of that. But when I got my first wages I went and bought a little miniature made in England. I never bought anything that was made in Australia, if I could help it. It took all my money. It was a tiny little English house all to remind me of England. I wanted to keep my identity with England. I felt if I had something English, there was still that hope. I've still got the prayer book that I brought out.

As if this was not enough to contend with, and despite the ruling that the girls were sent to "good Catholic families", the twenty-one year old son of the household tried to rape her.

I was going to the toilet one night. I had to take a torch to go down, it was down the back, a fair way from the house. And I was in my nightie and he met me coming back and he grabbed me and pulled me into his room. I assumed he was trying to rape me, I'm sure he was, but we didn't know anything about sex, we were told nothing about sex. Just don't ever let a man touch you. He tried to get m' legs apart, but I just crossed my legs and put my hands between me legs 'cause that was m' rude parts and you were brought up very strict and just didn't do anything down there.

He was trying to get my legs apart. I must have been quite strong, he kept me there for two hours. I was too scared to cry out 'cause I thought the rest of the family would accuse me. I knew they would blame me. And all the time I'm pleading, "Please don't touch me, don't hurt me, don't do anything wrong," begging him to let me go back to bed. I didn't know what he was going to do to me, but I knew it wasn't going to be very nice.

And the next morning his mother confronts me at the breakfast table, with all the family sitting round, and said, "Where were you last night?" She'd been checking on me, she always did. And I said, "In bed" and she said, "You were not. You were missing for two hours. You were up in the shearers' shed. You were up with the shearers, weren't you?" And that rotten son was sitting there saying, "I don't know how she could do it, how she could go, the trollop, how she could spend that time with the shearers," when he was the one who had me in his room.

I hated him after that. To me he was a horrible person. He used to chase me with dead snakes, lashing them at me. Any chance he got he'd try to get me. I'd go in to make his bed, and he'd sneak in very quietly – he was a great big strapping fellow. And he'd throw me on the bed. And the only thing I could think of was to cross my legs. Oh, I fought it! Oh yes! I got to the stage where I would wait until he was out of the house, shearing or doing something, and I'd race in to make his bed and out again. I was so scared. I can laugh about it now, but I didn't laugh in those days. I used to cry.

She was fifteen years old when this happened. She knew she had to leave the farm but she didn't know who to turn to. She was scared to tell the priest about the son and his attempts to rape her, in case he thought it was her fault, that she was seducing him. But after about a year she phoned the head of the Catholic welfare who had, she understood, originally placed her and said she hated her job, she was lonely and wanted to come back to Adelaide, to be near the other girls.

When I had my weekends off I would go back to Adelaide and stay with one of the girls down there. And she used to say, "Why don't you find a job here?" And I used to say, "Well I'm not allowed to, Father Roberts won't let me." She said, "Of course you can, you can do what you want." I knew full well I couldn't, so she went with me to see him the first time. But no, he was unbending. I had to stay on this farm, I had to work. I had to do this and do that.

Pamela phoned again.

And he threatened me with everything: "No you're not allowed to leave, you've got to stay there, you ungrateful girl." And I said, "No, I want to leave." I was crying every night. So eventually he gave in and said yes, I could come back to Adelaide.

Pamela did not have the confidence to leave the job without permission and simply go down to Adelaide on her own and get a job. She was afraid of what the priest would have done to her for being "uncontrollable". She, like others, had been brainwashed into doing what they were told ever since arriving in Australia.

You see, we were supposed to consider ourselves very lucky that they had found us a job, found us somewhere to live, a home where people could love us. Unfortunately the people didn't love us, they treated us as slaves.

Over the years, Pamela became increasingly obsessed about her lack of family.

I got to the stage where I thought there's just no hope, I'm never going to find anybody. But, you know, surely there must be somebody, somewhere that I'm related to, even if it's an aunt or an uncle. I got to the stage I was getting desperate, I didn't care. Just to have some identity. Because you feel as if you've got none – you're *nobody,* you're nothing. No roots at all.

I still resent the fact that someone could walk into a classroom in England, pluck you out, take you to Australia, with no prospect of ever coming back. You do this with animals, you sell them off, you cart them away. That's how I feel we were treated. I'd give my eye teeth to go back to see the place, to see England, to be there in April with all the beautiful flowers and trees. I resent the fact that my childhood's been taken away, never to be seen again . . . I have this feeling of loss and senselessness. How am I ever going to see England again, how am I going to find anybody all the way out here?

The Fairbridge Memorial College, situated in the bush outside Bulawayo in Zimbabwe was originally an RAF base. It opened to take the first group of children in 1946. The brochure pointed out that, "In Southern Rhodesia most of the manual tasks on farms are performed by the African." Rhodesia at that time was selective about immigrants. White children could not be expected to do manual work, but could consider themselves the "elite".

MIKE WILKINS went out there in 1949, aged seven, with a group of eleven boys and two girls, including his eight year old brother, Geoff. He is now an executive sales director, with a large house, an acre or so of land, a white BMW and a swimming pool. He says, "Fairbridge gave me the determination to succeed."

He and his brother, both of whom had been placed in a children's Home, went out after their father had applied to the Fairbridge scheme. Mike says his father did so "to give us kids a chance because he felt that no way were his children going to have a good future under the circumstances he found himself in [divorce]".

> He felt very guilty for what he did in the end. He did warn us what he was trying to do. Geoff was dead against it, even at that age. Being that year younger, I was all for it. I wanted to get the hell out of it: when you have a broken home, children can act very strangely.
>
> I remember we went to Rhodesia House twice. They explained where we were going, but it did not mean very much to me. They gave us blazers with a nice big F on the top. One of the criteria was intelligence and social standing, and I do know we had to pass a certain IQ and go through various tests.
>
> We sailed on the *Winchester Castle* and then came up from Cape Town by train, which took four or five days, and got to Bulawayo in late January. I will never forget arriving at Fairbridge. It was a Sunday morning, everyone running off to church. And someone said, "Here's a towel" and I remember jumping into the swimming pool, thinking it was Christmas, and the next thing I was being pulled out as I did not even know how to swim.
>
> In our own batch, there were children who were very homesick and had problems. But children of that age are very resilient, you were not going to be upset for very long. Some kids among us were very quiet, though, and stuck together like glue. There were some 120 children already there, they were coming out at regular intervals. It got so they were really banging them out. I think it's with hindsight that one starts thinking back that probably what they were doing is sending children out here to colonise. We were brought up like any other ordinary kids, but in an environment where schooling was strictly for white children.

As a junior, Mike went to school at Fairbridge itself; as a senior (from the age of twelve), he went to secondary school in Bulawayo.

> It was a long day as most of us had to travel in those very slow buses. Our school was miles away and that bus had to go to all the other schools to let children off. They spread us around; it wasn't a bad idea, Fairbridge had quite a forceful bunch of kids, pretty tough compared to the local children. No one ever wanted to come up against the Fairbridge guy, as they did not know how many others were behind him. We were taught to be very, very independent.
>
> I made a complete disaster of my schooling and passed no exams. Five of us left school together and went to work a hundred miles north

of Bulawayo at the Bata Shoe Company and only one of us managed to last. I was back at Fairbridge within three months and Fairbridge had a scheme – we nicknamed it the Rejects' Cottage – and you had a special table in the dining room until you sorted yourself out. Most kids would start their first job and things would go wrong. It was just somewhere to sleep and live. It was only once I got married that I woke up and realised I better get on with things. I married very young, a week before my twenty-first birthday. When you were twenty-one you were handed your birth certificate by Fairbridge, and any other documentation. It was a big stage in your life.

If there was such a term as a poor white, I don't think you will find it among Fairbridge people. Most had the will to go places. The girls were just like the guys. They were tough and I do believe we had all the opportunities. Things did not burn me up. It gave me the determination to succeed. In those days, a white definitely felt superior. I don't blame anyone for it. And the fact that I am still here means I can adjust to the present-day situation; the ones who couldn't see a future for themselves have left. But it's still a fantastic country, where you can make money.

3

The First Exodus

From 1618 to 1967 Britain continued to export its children. Today, eleven per cent of Canada's population is descended from these child migrants. The principal aim was to place the children in a colony or part of the Empire where they would stay and become citizens.

Most were selected for emigration because they were regarded at being at risk in some way – perhaps of being maltreated by their families or of becoming delinquents or beggars. Sometimes they were homeless "street arabs", as Dr Barnardo christened them, sometimes they had been placed in a Home. Some parents with family problems couldn't cope and handed over their children, temporarily or permanently, to various children's Homes or agencies, who then sent them overseas with or without their parents' knowledge or blessing. Sometimes they went direct from a parent's or relative's home. Almost all the children, once abroad, were placed in menial occupations: girls as domestic servants, boys as farm labourers. Separated from their own families, they were rarely adopted.

Today, child migration seems harsh, even barbaric and hard to justify. Yet justified it was, by governments in Britain and in the Empire. Colonial governments actively encouraged it, making grants of money or land to help establish it. In the 1880s, the Speaker of the New South Wales Legislative in Australia said, "We wish to receive [child] migration: we are willing to pay for them."

The movement of these children falls into approximately three periods. The first child migrants were sent to Australia, Canada, the USA, South Africa, Rhodesia, the West Indies and Bermuda. They mainly went out under the umbrella of local Boards of Guardians and were always greeted with open approval by the governments of the countries receiving them.

Starting in the 1860s was the era of the great philanthropists, or the "child-savers", as they are called. They were all empire-builders and Canada seemed to them the ideal place to send British children. They extolled her wide open spaces and the healthy farm life and Canada, in turn, welcomed farm labour – whatever age the labourer. Ontario wanted as many non-Catholics as possible to settle there, conscious of Catholic expansion in the adjacent province of Quebec and Quebec, eyeing the influx, called in turn for child Catholics. But with the onset of the Depression in the mid 1920s, Canada announced it would no longer accept unaccompanied children.

The upheavals of the Second World War resulted in post-war marriage breakdowns and a sharp rise in illegitimacy. Many children were placed in Homes, often with the request that they be adopted. It was these children who were shipped off in their thousands, mostly to Australia. They are still alive and have a clear memory of the events and emotions they felt, as well as being living examples of the long-term after-effects.

In the year 1618, the Virginia Company in America – short of labour and desperate to increase its British population – asked the Burghers of the City of London to send over some of its unwanted children. They agreed and, later that year, a hundred such children crossed the Atlantic to Virginia, the very first child migrants to leave Britain. It must have been a dangerous journey, as mortality on emigrant ships from Liverpool to the North American provinces was high. Throughout the seventeenth century, small groups of "unwanted" children continued to be sent out, usually to America but sometimes to the West Indies. The cost of the voyage, or perhaps the cost of a set of clothes, was sometimes paid for by private donations from philanthropists, but mostly costs were borne by the Boards of Guardians who, under the Poor Law, were elected by ratepayers to administer public relief to the destitute. They were therefore eager to offload pauper children to ease the burden on the rates.

In the eighteenth century, child migration was bound up with a different policy: the transportation of convicted felons, mostly to the colonies. Under common law, an offender could be prosecuted from the age of seven years old, and children were transported right up to the early part of the nineteenth century. Usually, however, transported child migrants had not been convicted of offences, they were just considered potential trouble-makers. In an 1826 report on emigration from the United Kingdom, a Mr R. J. Chambers, a Metropolitan police magistrate, expressed a general opinion when he said:

I conceive that London has become too full of children. There has been a great increase of juvenile offences, which I attribute to want of employment for people between the ages of twelve and twenty. I therefore suggest emigration as a remedy.

It was because of the transportation policy, which ended for children in 1853, that Edward Brenton, a retired naval captain, developed a scheme for child migrants which was more enlightened. Brenton thought that family neglect was one of the main explanations for child delinquency and that there was little hope of change unless such children could earn their living respectably. This meant learning a trade. He also thought they would never respond to such training if they were badly treated, believing brutal treatment produced brutalised captives who were unwilling to learn.

To carry out his ideas, Edward Brenton founded a society called the Society for the Suppression of Juvenile Vagrancy. (The name was later changed to the Children's Friend Society.) Its aim was to promote emigration among destitute children by training them in two Homes, the Brenton Juvenile Asylum at Hackney (for boys) and the Royal Victoria Asylum at Chiswick (for girls). It offered a home to children who were living from begging and stealing; assisted parishes in managing and disposing of their "refractory" children; and offered to help respectable families whose children had been trapped into working for the "Fagins" of the time.

There was, for those times, relatively little punishment in Brenton's Homes. Flogging was strictly forbidden and solitary confinement for stealing offences lasted only six or seven hours. Yet the Homes were not holiday camps and they demanded strict discipline and prompt obedience. The object was to teach them to look after themselves: grind their own corn, cook their own meals and learn the skills necessary for colonial emigration. By the mid 1830s, Brenton was sending children to Canada, Australia and, above all, South Africa. The aim was to apprentice them to "respectable" people.

Although Brenton was mainly concerned with delinquent children, he was also anxious to care for the poor and the destitute in order to prevent them, in turn, becoming delinquent. His method was clear: a firm but severe hand, with adequate social and moral training. In fact, because the luxurious habits of the South African "Cape colonists" were thought to threaten the moral well-being of the children, Canada, whose farmers led a simpler life, overtook South Africa as the main destination.

Brenton was the first to realise that once the children arrived in a new country, they would need lengthly supervision. By 1835, a committee had been set up in Cape Town to oversee both girls and boys on arrival, supervise their apprenticeship and ensure they were well cared for. It was a sound move which those involved with child migration over the next century mostly failed to match.

But Brenton had adversaries and his Society was accused of ill treating and neglecting the children. Lord John Russell, then Colonial Secretary, instructed Sir George Napier, the Governor of Cape Colony, to set up an inquiry into the condition of the young migrants.

The report, which he submitted on 24 February 1840, came to the general conclusion that any anxieties were "in a great measure groundless". However, not all aspects of the report were favourable and the loneliness and isolation of many of the children came through clearly – despite the much-flaunted inspections. Take the following cases:

I am about eighteen and a half years old: my master, when I was indentured to him was a baker in Cape Town, at which trade I continued about 11 months when my master gave it up and became a travelling hawker through the interior of the colony selling and exchanging soft goods etc. for sheep and cattle. I accompanied him on three journeys which I found extremely fatiguing, having to walk back from the other extremity of the colony each time carrying a pack on my back, driving the sheep down to the part of the colony to market: there were always two or three coloured servants who treated me very ill . . . beating me severely if any things went wrong, and for these reasons, when my master last set out again on a similar journey, about 6 months ago, I requested him to leave me behind, which he consented to, on condition that I should maintain and provide for myself during his absence and pay him besides 6 dollars per month and I have done so except for 2 months that I was sick and unable to earn my money . . . I should wish to learn a trade or go back to England, I have an elder brother living there.   *William Henry Evett*

I am about 15 years old: my parents are living in England: I cannot read or write; my general health is good but am much troubled with sores on my neck; never go to church but hear the family prayers at home. I can't speak English now. I am employed nursing or house-work; sleep in the same apartment with my mistress; have no complaints to make.   *Sarah Piper*

I am about 15 years old; my mother is living in England: cannot read or write; never go to church; am employed as a farm labourer and herding cattle: had a letter from my mother some time back and my master answered it for me; I wish to get back to her.   *Charles Boyce*

The commissioners stressed that the report must be set against the current condition of the children and their background, "Many of these children were either in, or bordering on, a state of depravity when they were initially reclaimed, and many were indentured in country districts where the means of attending divine worship was not available." In the circumstances, depravity was all too likely – the more so considering "these juvenile immigrants were on their arrival apprenticed and domiciled with persons of loose habits and moral observances and careless of a sense of moral obligation". But on the brighter side, it was also reported that:

> Comparing the [children's] appearances now with what they were when they arrived – ie, that many of them have been stunted in their growth by the treatment they receive in the colony – the impression on our minds is that the physical condition of these children has been decidedly improved in all aspects since their arrival here.

The most thoughtful, though strong criticism came from one H. Piers. He said he thought the children were generally healthy, well-clothed and well-treated, with some obvious exceptions. He noted that most of them had been placed in Afrikaans-speaking households, where there was no religious instruction, so that children like Sarah Piper were fast losing their religion and language. He was also concerned that if children were not apprenticed properly, they would "continue in the same degraded, hopeless condition of a farm labourer without a chance that I can perceive of their ever rising higher".

In contrast, those apprenticed to tradesmen like carpenters, masons and so on, had a much brighter future: they learnt their trades, did not mix with the local labouring classes, received religious instruction and did not live in the isolated country districts where there was no school instruction. Piers concluded, "They may also reasonably, I think, look forward to becoming masters in their turn."

Sir George Napier wasn't at all pleased about the inquiry. He considered it had led to "the strongest disinclination on the part of local Commissioners to receive and take charge of any more children".

Many of Edward Brenton's hopes for delinquent children became reality in Britain in the next decade when separate prisons were introduced for juvenile offenders and transportation ended. Some young offenders were offered the chance of emigrating to the colonies rather than staying in an English prison as an incentive to behave well.

Children from one juvenile prison, Parkhurst, along with others from certain reformatory schools, were sent overseas and this added to the steady number of children sent to the colonies. In 1848, the London Ragged Schools sent out 150 boys and girls to Australia, and continued to send out roughly that amount every year until the early 1860s. The Philanthropic Society Farm School in Redhill sent an annual contingent of fifty children, and Mary Carpenter, one of the many Victorian reformers eager to deal with the problem of delinquent children, also began to send children overseas, though not on the scale of later reformers.

It was as transportation for juvenile offenders was coming to an end that people began to be more conscious of children's welfare. Nevertheless, almost any plan would do if it could be argued that it was in the child's best interests. And ironically, as this era in the history of transportation came to an end, the great era of child migration for non-offenders began. It is a pattern that still repeats itself today: whenever policies are rejected – like transportation because it was thought too harsh – new projects turn up that are based on the same ideas as those they are replacing. So when child migration replaced transportation, children were sent to the same sorts of places – even if in less harsh surroundings.

Why was child migration thought worthwhile? The reasons for sending children reappear over the next hundred years or so: they were partly political, partly economic and partly philanthropic.

First, the political issues. In the 1850s, Britain was immensely keen to populate the colonies. The colonies, in turn, wanted to increase their numbers with European stock – especially British stock. Child migration was therefore just one part of the whole picture of emigration. In Victorian society, moral duty was regarded as part of the Englishman's burden and colonisation came under that heading. Its object, according to an 1850 Commons debate on emigration, was to encourage a proper class of emigrant.

Emigration figures were boosted by certain events. The years up to 1850 were the years immediately after the potato famine in Ireland, for instance; 1848–9 was a period of revolutionary upheaval in Europe. Altogether 805,867 people emigrated from the United Kingdom from 1847 to 1850, with 56,000 going to Australia and New Zealand. The entire population of these two countries was only 326,000.

Another political factor was fear of unrest in the colonies. Here child migration had two outstanding advantages. First, young children could be moulded into good colonial citizens and, secondly, girls could be sent out to offset the colonies' constant and desperate shortage of women. It was constantly emphasised that the younger the children on arrival, the better citizens they became. The Australian, Captain Stanley Carr (described as a gentleman of great experience), was recorded in *Hansard* as saying that, "The emigration of pauper children is preferable to that of adults." And in a report to the Emigration Commission, a Mr

Cooper said that children brought up in properly managed workhouses were more intelligent "and equally as able to earn their livelihood by labour as when brought up by parents".

Even though girls were often disparagingly and officially described as "a species of female emigrants", they were needed not only as wives but to act as domestic servants. Most girls were hired for this job while still on board, long before the ship arrived, and some weren't always suitable. In 1847, for instance, a group of girls from Belfast and another group from Marylebone caused a lot of trouble on the voyage to Australia. It was alleged the Belfast girls, fifty-three "orphans" who travelled to Australia on the *Earl Grey,* were actually prostitutes! Supporters of the Belfast girls insisted they were of good character and that any misbehaviour was the fault of some of the officials on board; while the Marylebone women were castigated as "fiends in human shape", a nuisance to all and users of the most disgraceful and disgusting language. According to *Hansard*: "It was stated they could not be kept from the sailors and that they almost excited the crew to mutiny. The Belfast girls were purity itself when compared with these Marylebone ladies."

From an economic point of view, sending children out to the colonies benefited Britain in a number of ways. There was the cost to the State of keeping children. The children concerned were "destitute foundlings", and were defined as having no parents, or one parent who couldn't or wouldn't care for the child. Victorians were very anxious that the Poor Law wasn't burdened unnecessarily.

The children themselves were rarely considered: if they were, it was just a question of whether younger children were preferable to older ones, girls preferable to boys or independent children preferable to docile ones. No one cared if they were lonely, homesick for their parents and families or wanted family information. These charitable remarks made by a churchwarden in 1852 underline the general attitude:

> The cost of maintaining and educating such children is at the rate of 3s. 6d. a week each. We cannot put them out to service till they are fourteen. They are soon returned upon our hands: the girls in many cases pregnant. They often marry at an early age, and begat a race of paupers . . .

The Boards of Guardians calculated that emigration cost the equivalent of a year's maintenance in a parish workhouse, so a child sent abroad at seven saved the parish six years' keep. As the cost of passage was subsidised through the Poor Law Fund, this made an even higher saving.

It was the 1850 Poor Law Amendment Act that gave the Guardians legal authority to send children under sixteen overseas. Under Section 5 of the Act, the Guardians of any union or parish could "procure or assist the emigration of any poor person", and charge the cost to the common fund. The Act was said to carry too many limitations because the child had to have his/her application submitted to the Poor Law Board for approval, together with a Certificate of Consent backed by two justices. But what was more of a problem was raising funds. Here the 1849 Irish Act scored – it allowed Boards of Guardians to raise emigration money on the rates.

An extract from the *Morning Chronicle* of 18 January 1851 shows how certain London Boards of Guardians saved money by handing their child charges over to unscrupulous sea captains, paying so little for the cost of their passage that the captains were virtually operating a slave trade to make a profit:

Marylebone Board of Guardians. At the weekly meeting of the Guardians yesterday . . . Captain Burrows, of the brig *James,* gave an account of the boys and girls from the workhouse conveyed by him to Bermuda as emigrants. The following questions were put to the captain:

Question: What must be the ages of the children?
Answer: Between twelve and fourteen.
Q: What do you do with them when you get them to Bermuda?
A: I apprentice them as domestic servants until they are eighteen.
Q: On what conditions do you take them?
A: I charge six shillings passage money, for which I find them bed, bedding, and board. The parish provides their outfit.
Q: After they serve their apprenticeship what becomes of them?
A: Why, they get other situations.
Q: Are there any funds to assist them in getting situations or returning home, if they desire it, after their apprenticeship?
A: No, sir. I have taken out sixty children from St. Pancras Workhouse . . .
Q: Have you a female to attend them on board?
A: The last time I went out there was in the cabin a female passenger aged nineteen.
Q: That was accidental?
A: Yes, sir.
Q: Suppose you can't get situations for them when they reach Bermuda, what do you do?
A: I engage to provide them with situations; I have places for them all . . .
Q: You have stated that you have had sent you from the sixty children from St. Pancras original letters in which they speak highly of their comforts. Surely you can produce thirty of these letters?
A: They are with the master of St. Pancras Workhouse.

Q: When do you sail?
A: On the 25th [eight days after the date of the meetings].
Q: How many children will you take?
A: As many as you please. *(Laughter)*

Some MPs wanted to save both on the existing Poor Law children *and* on the future cost of the Poor Law. (By the 1860s, the annual increase in British paupers was around seven per cent, a high cost to the Poor Law.) They wanted to send other children, including "children of widows not in the workhouse, children of widowers not in the workhouse, who with the consent of their parents might emigrate to some advantage". Others did not share their enthusiasm but some fifteen or twenty years later, such children were sent abroad by the great Victorian philanthropists for precisely the same reasons.

The colonies had their own economic reasons for taking these children. They wanted new stock and a ready supply of labour. Many emigrants were small farmers and entrepreneurs and they and their wives needed domestic servants and help. Child migrants were ideal for their needs. It seemed perfectly natural that pauper children should provide the colonies with the "benefits of servitude". What is extraordinary is that this type of thinking persisted. It could be seen in Dr Barnardo's child migration scheme, Annie Macpherson's and, in the twentieth century, that of Kingsley Fairbridge. The Fairbridge Farm Schools saw their task as providing a steady supply of farm labourers and domestic servants for the colonies. Child migration was not just about moving children from one society in Britain to another, overseas. It was about taking certain types of children and rearing them to fill certain positions in that society. This was bitterly and understandably resented by the children, particularly by post-Second World War migrants, who say that one of the hardest things they had to bear was the view that they were there to be servants for others.

By 1860, many more children were being shipped abroad and concern about their plight was slowly starting to surface. In 1861, *Hansard* recorded a Mr Senior saying:

> We look with shame and indignation at the pictures of American slavery, but I firmly believe that the children at the worst managed plantations are less overworked, less tortured, better fed, and quite as well instructed as the unhappy infants whose early and long continued labour occasions the fabulous cheapness of our hardware . . .

Other parliamentary critics of child migration said the Poor Law Guardians were failing in their duty when they sent young, unprotected children abroad, with no after-care provision. They argued that it was pointless "sending out any large portion of our pauper children who would not find themselves on arrival in a different and much better condition to that which they would occupy in this country".

It was the beginning of an awareness of the inherent dangers in child migration and the shift was evident when the earnest social reformer, the Earl of Shaftesbury, tried to pass the Pauper Children Emigration Bill in the Lords on 26 June 1852. Shaftesbury supported child migration and the Bill was to allow parishes or Boards of Guardians to raise funds for this purpose. He wanted to send more and younger girls "in order to fit them by an education of not less than a year to become useful servants and eligible wives". As patron of the Ragged Schools, he had already sent children to Australia.

The Earl of Derby was the most forthright critic of the Bill. In a speech to the House, he said:

> I wish to impress upon the noble Earl that he ought to be exceedingly cautious in dealing with this matter. It was of the utmost importance that the greatest precaution should be taken as the mode in which these children should be disposed of on their arrival in the colonies, because several benevolent plans, founded on social principles, had already been devised for the same object as that which my noble friend has in view, but they had led, when put into execution, to results of a very painful description, and the public mind had thereby become much prejudiced against them.

The bill was withdrawn. But although the Earl of Derby won that particular battle, he and other opponents of child migration were to lose many more.

So the first era of child migration was drawing to an end. It had lasted some 250 years and had grown steadily: 500 to 1,000 children a year were shipped overseas in the last fifty or so years of this period. Between 1800–1850 most children went to Australia. The Canadian market then started to take over from Australia which was only to resurface properly after the Second World War. When New Zealand became a British colony in 1840 small numbers of children were sent there.

In the next decade or so the private philanthropists were to take over, sending far more children than the Poor Law Guardians ever dreamt of. It was these private philanthropists, organised and full of energy, who were responsible for the extraordinary expansion of the child migration scheme.

4

"The Child-savers"

In the 1950s, a poster from the Fairbridge Society showed a slum child in Britain gazing at an outline of Australia in the sky. His loneliness could, it seems, only be relieved by emigration. The plea for funds comes next: "Help him join his friends", is the message. The attractions of the wide open spaces were fervently endorsed by the private philanthropists. It stemmed from a belief, fondly held by the Victorians, that urban areas and particularly the larger cities, produced moral degeneracy and polluted the very soul. Only the pure, ennobling life of the countryside could cleanse and purify.

The idea actually came from Germany. After the 1849 revolutions, two German Protestants started to place destitute and criminal youngsters in the countryside, away from the ungodly, radical politics of the cities. The British pounced on the idea: they could send their destitute children to colonial farms, where agricultural work was purifying and rural life innocent and godly.

Charles Devonport remembers the purity of rural life being stressed when Canada was first suggested to him:

> This Captain Hind got up on the stage where we had been watching a movie. There were twelve hundred boys in uniform, blue uniforms with silver buttons, black leather belts and a strap and a little pillbox hat with white stripes and two silver buttons. To attend the movie you had to be properly dressed. And he said, "I'd like to have twelve boys, more or less, to go to Canada, who really want to go", and he stressed the advantages, the fresh air, away from the pollution, learning how to farm, and become citizens who would carry the flag, the British tradition, overseas.

At the peak of the second phase of child migration – 1870 to 1925 – at least twenty-five large philanthropic organisations were sending children to Canada. Why Canada? Why not continue with Australia or New Zealand?

Canada was seen as safer. In her book, *Children of the Empire*, Gillian Wagner says that children weren't sent to Australia after

1853 because of the gold rush. Apart from possible contamination from the diggings, "many of the boys would be susceptible to the contagion of those moral diseases which have broken out in the train of gold fever". Also the passage to Canada cost much less and Canada had an insatiable demand for labour.

About 100,000 British children were sent to Canada during this time. They were rarely adopted or officially fostered and hardly a third were genuine orphans. "Most were not yet fourteen and still too young for full time employment in the UK, although their educational opportunities would be limited in Canada and their work heavy," says Joy Parr, in *Labouring Children,* adding dryly, "It seems strange to find such a policy flourishing in the late nineteenth and twentieth century."

Education was undoubtedly limited. Employers signed a contract or agreement laying down ground rules and some of these specified there would be no education at all in the summer (when farmers were particularly busy). But whatever the season, employers weren't interested in education. George Barrett, who went out to Canada in 1922 at the age of twelve to work on a farm, remembers his few schooldays well.

> In the winter time I never went to school. I only went to school two summers, the only education I got in Canada. When you first came to school, you had an [English] accent and they laughed at you. I had to run half a mile to the school, which was a one-room schoolhouse, with outside toilets, with partitions, a tin cup and bucket hanging on the wall for our drinking water, and an old wood stove. The school board paid fifteen cents for a boy or girl to start the fire and at twelve noon I would have to run home to my farm, eat dinner and go out and feed cattle. He [the farmer] used to hire a chap to cut the year's corn and I had to turn the grindstone to turn the axe. And he would keep me until five to one and I had to run to school and would be late. He would laugh and I remember he had boils and I used to say, "I hope those boils will kill you".

Bert Wayling, who was thirteen when sent to Canada in the 1920s through Dr Barnardo's, remembers his first day at school being a disaster:

> After breakfast I was told to change my clothes and go to the school, which was about a mile and a half up the road, which was made of clay. The clay was of a white or yellow colour and had all the qualities of a good glue. I was wearing the clothes that I wore on the trip over, which were the jacket, knee pants, black shoes and stockings. By the time I arrived at the school, I could hardly drag one foot ahead of the other and I was mud up to my knees.

The schoolhouse was a fairly small one-room building with a playground in front. A group of kids were playing together and to my dismay I realised that they were all dressed in overalls and rubber boots and here I was dressed up like little Lord Fauntleroy. Of course as soon as I got in there they stopped and looked at me as if someone from outer space had arrived. We stared at each other for what seemed like hours to me, before I screwed up enough courage to speak, and then not having learned to speak Canadian yet, I spoke to them in English and said, "Hello, there." This finally broke them up in great gales of laughter.

The teacher looked at me, but she was more or less indifferent. But I got into trouble when I got back home for fighting and the mud. The next day I refused to go back to school with little Lord Fauntleroy clothes and they bought me farm clothes.

The widow of another child migrant, George Plume, who came out to Ontario when he was ten, also through Dr Barnardo's, said:

After George's first two months at school, the teacher suggested to George's boss that she come to the farm two nights a week to give George lessons. She was told the boy was there to work and not to be made a gentleman.

Dr Barnardo was the most influential figure in the child migration of the period and his organisation the most important. The first Barnardo party of fifty children, aged between fourteen and seventeen, set sail for Canada in 1882. Another group of a hundred boys went off in June, 1883, and the first group of seventy-two girls left Liverpool for Ontario a month later: the youngest being just four years old. Altogether, Dr Barnardo's organisation sent over 20,000 children to Canada between 1882 and 1914.

It was an impressive scheme. Barnardo had a genuine concern for children and tried to produce and enforce a system of inspection and after-care. This is shown in a lengthy leaflet put out by Barnardo's first Canadian branch:

Any person taking a boy will be required to sign an undertaking, in duplicate, at the time the boy is sent, engaging to provide for his maintenance and education, to send him regularly to Church and Sunday School, and to communicate periodically with the Agent of the Home, and otherwise to care for and to promote the boy's interests.

Boys who are boarded-out will be regularly visited by a representative of the Home, and the undertaking above-mentioned contains a stipulation that every facility will be afforded this representative to make such inspection as he may consider necessary to satisfy himself that the conditions of the undertaking are being faithfully fulfilled.

It is hoped that every effort will be made on the part of those who take boys to train them in habits of truthfulness, obedience, and personal cleanliness and industry. With this object, they should be accustomed as soon as possible to take part in the work of the farm, but it is pointed out that it would be manifestly contrary to the spirit of the undertaking to require from them any hard or laborious work while their maintenance is being paid for, and moreover, their constant and regular attendance at school must be insisted upon during the time the undertaking remains in force.

Despite the promises, the long distances, the hard Canadian winters and the sheer numbers of children involved made adequate inspection impossible. Annie Smith, sent out to Canada through Middlemore Homes, was sexually harassed by the two sons of the farmer but found it impossible to confide in the Middlemore inspector.

Once a year they came and visited us. I did not tell them, it seemed as though they did not want you to say anything, they would keep talking about this, that and the other; they never asked you anything to give you a chance to tell them anything.

When Annie was finally rescued by the farmer's sister, she heard the sister tell the Home that "it was a shame that Annie had to go through those first two years. This person [the inspector, Mrs Ray] should have investigated more." Annie recalled that:

Mrs Ray did not know where to put herself and she just made excuses, she said they did not have time as they had to visit so many each day and there was such a distance between each one that they just couldn't put all that time into finding out the ins and outs. I don't think they wanted to, myself. They just did not want to be *bothered*.

Joy Parr says that nine per cent of boys and fifteen per cent of girls from Barnardo's Homes were treated so badly by the employers that they had to be taken away. The employers were reprimanded but only when (or if) the assaults were discovered.

The Barnardo organisation stated in 1988 that its policy of sending children abroad was just part of an historical era, a stage in its development, which it said would be entirely inappropriate today. But why did Barnardo ever become involved with child migrants?

Thomas John Barnardo, always known as Dr Barnardo though he qualified only later in life, was born on 4 July 1845 in Dublin. His father was of Jewish origin and his mother an Irish Catholic; but Barnardo liked to imply that his father had a Lutheran past and his mother was a Quaker. Despite living in Dublin, the earnest and devout family was Protestant. In 1862, at seventeen, Barnardo became a convert to evangelical Christianity, some argued a religious zealot. He believed his calling was to be a missionary in China. Energetic, opinionated and sure of his acceptance, he had already started to study medicine, thinking it would be valuable for his missionary work overseas, but to his surprise, he was rejected as unsuitable (he was considered too headstrong) by the China Island Mission. He was, at this time, already preaching on the streets of the East End and was soon influenced by a woman called Annie Macpherson, who had recently started sending children to Canada. His first contact with destitute children was to pray for their souls – concern over their clothing and shelter came later, when he founded a mission for children in the East End.

One night in 1872 he met Jim Jarvis, when he, like other children, refused to leave the warmth of the mission. Barnardo, telling him to run off, described the scene in *The Christian*:

> "Got no home," was the boy's quick rejoinder. "Got no home! Be off and go home to your mother; don't tell me!" – "Got no mother," repeated the boy. "Then go home to your father." – "Got no father," said the little fellow. "Got no father! But where are your friends? Where do you live?" – "Don't live nowhere; got no friends," said the lonely lad.

Barnardo heard that there were more children in this situation than the boy could count, all scavenging, begging and stealing. But what really shocked him was that when he asked the child if he had ever heard of Jesus, the reply was, "He's the Pope of Rome." That to Barnardo was enough. His distrust of Roman Catholicism spurred on his efforts to save these children and his dream of missionary work in China ended. That night, Barnardo took his first child, Jim Jarvis, into care. Later, Jim became one of the first child migrants.

By the time Barnardo became involved in child migration, he was already established as the foremost philanthropist and child care expert. Still not thirty-five, he had a juvenile mission in the East End, schools throughout London attended by hundreds of children and numerous children's Homes and orphanages. Phyllis Dorey's eighty-year-old memories of the Barnardo's Home in Barkingside, were that:

> It was not *too* bad. But the meals were terrible. It was very strict and the floors had to be scrubbed and the table tops. Everybody had their own job to do: one scrubbed and one washed. It was the same at the Dr Barnardo's Home for girls in Peterborough, Ontario, you had to scrub floors and things there.

Barnardo was clearly aware of public criticism of child migration. He gives his reasons for becoming involved with it in his *Memoirs*:

> Well-planned and wisely conducted child-emigration, especially to Canada, contains within its bosom the truest solution of some of the mother-country's most perplexing problems, and the supply of our Colonies' most urgent needs . . . First, it relieves the overcrowded centres of city life and the congested labour-markets at home, while, at the same time, it lessens in a remarkable manner the burdens of taxation. Second, it supplies what the Colonies are most in want of – an increase of the English-speaking population . . . Third, it confers upon the children themselves unspeakable blessings . . .
>
> I regard with amazement . . . the unwillingness of a great administrative department of the State to sanction a small expenditure for the maintenance of its child-clients in one of our Colonies *at half the annual cost that is already being incurred in maintaining the same children in England* . . .

The question of costs was dear to Barnardo's heart. He was only too aware that keeping children in institutions was expensive and as he relied on charitable gifts, he was always keen to keep costs down. Child migration offered a solution: more children could be taken in and cared for at less expense. What finally convinced him was the promise of a large donation if he opened a centre in Canada.

With economic depression in Britain escalating in the 1880s, Barnardo had an attentive audience when he claimed that, "Every boy rescued from the gutter is one dangerous man the less: each girl saved from a criminal course is a present to the next generation of a virtuous woman and a valuable servant." Helped by large donations, the Barnardo scheme really began and was to dominate all the others. When the Canadian market started to dry up after the 1924 Bondfield inquiry decided that child migrants of under fourteen should not be allowed to leave Britain, it simply transferred to Australia.

Barnardo often spoke of the Golden Bridge spanning the Atlantic Ocean between Britain and Canada. Over it, he said, would go thousands of children with high expectations, and over it they went, dressed neatly in their Barnardo's uniforms, always loyal to the man who saved them. It seems they never blamed Barnardo or his organisation when these same expectations were not fulfilled. Again and again child migrants are on record as saying that they held no bitterness, that Barnardo's did them no harm and maybe some good, and they thank him or his organisation for the help they gave.

Nevertheless, some children were unhappy enough to run away from the farmers they worked for. One young boy managed to stowaway on a ship leaving for England, and jumped ship when it got to Liverpool harbour – spending the rest of his life in that city. Others left and were simply never heard of again. As Phyllis Harrison says in her book on child migrants in Canada, *The Home Children*:

> To discourage boys from running away from employers, a condition that must have reached epidemic proportions at the height of the emigration of children, 1880–1914, medals were given to boys by some Homes. The Barnardo medal indicated these were given for "Long service and good conduct", but the qualification, in fact, was that the boy had served out his time at his original placement. No case of a girl receiving a medal has been traced . . . Yet the girls were as vulnerable as boys to abuse, although of a different kind. If they were less likely to feel a horsewhip across their backs, they were vulnerable to the sexual advances of their employer, his son, or in some cases, a hired man.

Always the showman and always keen to present the good side, Barnardo claimed that it was his children in Canada who were most in demand, his boys who were "far and away superior both as to physique and training and general deportment to any they had hitherto seen". He painted a glowing picture of the children's life in Canada and spoke poignantly of the children in Britain begging to go to Canada. "Please may I go to Canada is the most popular sentence just now on the lips of our girls – it comes even from tiny ones of four and five."

Even if they weren't begging to go, they were still sent. Phyllis Dorey, who left for Canada in 1915, at the age of eleven, says, "They just said, 'You are going to Canada,' and that was it. If you don't have a mother or father, who are you going to ask, you are just a child."

One boy who was thirteen when he left Barnardo's Boys' Garden City at Woodford Bridge, remembers being called into the main office:

> We were greeted by two gentlemen who informed us that we would be sent to another country in the near future. It was explained to us that the opportunities for a happy and prosperous life would be much better, and we would be living on a farm which would be both healthy and interesting. We were given the choice of three countries to which we might choose to be sent. Actually, we did not wish to be sent anywhere, at least speaking for myself. I was quite content to stay in jolly good England or merrie old England, even though England had not been so jolly or merrie of late. I still would rather have stayed there

than go to a strange country among strange people and strange customs. It had not dawned on me as yet that my sister was not going with me.

Another Barnardo boy said:

Kids in those days were regarded as a little less than human. They were sent to countries for economic reasons. It couldn't have been for the children's sake, not if they had any sensitivity at all.

Children hardly had a chance even to say goodbye to any member of their family. The rules of the Barnardo's Home in Woodford Bridge, Essex, show just how little contact was allowed:

VISITING DAYS for Parents and Friends of the Boys are the Second Saturdays of January, April, July and October from Two to Five o'clock.
LETTERS. Boys are allowed to receive letters at any time and to write to their friends BUT MUST PROVIDE THEIR OWN POSTAGE STAMPS.

One boy, who went to the Woodford Bridge Home, remembers his sister coming to visit him there for the last time.

She would stand there for two hours, at the fence that separated us. The only time my sister got in was just before I left for Canada and we went out and had tea. All she could do was exhort me to be a good boy; she was very upset that I was going. She died when I was nineteen. I never saw her again.

These children knew nothing of Canada, its climate, its people or what was expected of them. Even today, some sixty, seventy or eighty years after going to Canada, child migrants clearly remember their bewilderment. Bert Wayling looks back years to his arrival with thirty-five other Barnardo boys, and his general ignorance about the country:

After the business of customs was completed, we were marched up the street a short distance to the railroad station and there we got another surprise. A train was standing in the station and it looked like a huge building, the engine alone was gigantic compared to the engines we were used to, the size of the coaches simply took our breath away. It took a long while to go from St John's, New Brunswick, to Toronto, but we amused ourselves by watching the scenery as it was all quite new.
We all knew about rubber trees, and when we saw some trees with buckets hanging on them, our first thoughts were of rubber trees. In

those days England was at the head of a considerable empire and we were expected to know the basics of each member country. Somehow we must have missed Canada. We found out later that we had arrived in the midst of maple sugar making time and these were sap buckets!

We were a rather subdued bunch of boys for the remainder of the trip, no doubt wondering just what was in store for us, just what kind of people we would be living with and exactly just what kind of life it would be. Everything was so different to what we were used to. We were still more or less in shock as a result of what was already taking place. It was all too sudden, and all too severe a change.

There seemed to be a marked show of indifference toward us. This was something that always puzzled me. There was never any show of compassion by any of the people that we met in those first days in Canada. Maybe I expected something that was not really due. I don't ever remember anyone touching a boy in an affectionate way and some of the boys were quite small.

After we were there a couple of weeks, the boys started to be moved out. I was taken to the Union Station in downtown Toronto and turned over to a railway employee with no wish of good luck or a goodbye of any nature. He told me that the conductor would tell me when to get off and for this piece of information I was truly grateful, as I didn't have a clue where I was, or where I was going. By this time I was completely confused, scared and very lonely and homesick.

Each station we passed gave me some cause to worry, as I was afraid that the conductor would forget me and I would miss my stop and God knows where I would wind up. But the conductor put me off the train and took me over to an elderly looking gentleman and left. This gentleman looked me over and said, "Well, boy, if you work hard and behave yourself, you will have a good home." This was the first joyous greeting that I received. This guy was not concerned as to whether I was hungry or tired or upset, or even whether I needed to go to the bathroom, which it so happened that I did and quite badly too. I hadn't realised that there were toilets on the train. I still had a lot to learn about this strange country.

George Linsdell was sent to a farm near Guelph, Ontario.

But the farmer took one look at me, I was eleven years old, and said I was too small for the farm and put me back on the train. Then I went off by train again, and the people I went to picked me up and took me to their farm about three miles west of Omanee [Ontario]. I stayed there until I was eighteen, they housed me good. But there were a lot of kids from Barnardo's throughout this part of the country and a lot were not used well at all.

As far as Barnardo was concerned, however, by coming out to Canada, the children would have "the almost incalculable advantages conferred upon them by emigration". They would receive "pure, healthy surroundings where vice, drunkenness and harsh treatment are unknown. Homes too where family life and religious life are a blessed reality situated in a fair garden-like country."

The children had little option but to praise the blessed reality. Joy Parr says that tampering with the children's mail in Canada was regarded as all-important not only by Barnardo's but by the other philanthropic societies. Offending passages or pleas to return were deleted. Cleansed of criticism, their letters back to the institutions in England were proudly run in the magazines of the different societies.

I have a fine place here and have got a rise in my wages. I thank you very much for your kind advice. You may depend upon it that I shall never forget the home from which I got my start in life.

I am getting along very well and have a good home. I am now seventeen years old and go to Sunday School. I am going to try and be a better Christian.

I often think if you have forgot the time I blowed my shoeblack box to pieces with the fire cracker. I remember it as if it were to-day. I am above shoeblacking now, Thank God!

In the first five years, Barnardo's girls moved on average four times and the boys three times. Publicly, Barnardo said that the child migrants moved from one home to another to suit themselves and obtain "family life". But what often happened was that children would work for their board until they were fourteen, at which age they started to get paid for their work. Farmers would keep them until this age and then return them to the Home, not wanting to pay a wage, and ask for a younger child. And so the process would start again. If they were not suitable, their employer also returned them. Phyllis Dorey says her first posting ended in this hurtful way:

I was sent from the Dr Barnardo's Home in Peterborough to Toronto. They would call you in and say, "You are going to be placed in such and such a home tomorrow or the next day." No one took me, I went on my own because at that time there was a Travellers Aid in the station and they would come and meet you when you got off the train. In Toronto I went to the president of a car tyre company. They wanted to adopt a girl, but I guess I wasn't up to it, or what they wanted. When people did not want you, they called the Home or wrote to them and wanted you to go back to the Home. *You* did not have any say in it.

Barnardo was aware that there were two main criticisms of child migration: first, the selection procedures in Canada; secondly, the supervision of the children after selection. He tried to counter some of these criticisms, though he couldn't manage to refute them all. He produced a charter, which tried to offer a guarantee to the children and the Canadians who took them. It said that: only the flower of the flock were to be sent to Canada; children must be carefully trained; they must be under a qualified person; none with criminal or vicious traits could be sent or they would be returned home; that they must have good health.

It was one of Barnardo's constant themes that "only the flower of the flock" was sent to Canada, after training. But there's no evidence that his selection procedures were that rigorous. Children were sent out to Canada with relatively little notice or training. One child migrant remembers being in a Barnardo's Home in the East End for about a week before being shipped out to Canada with about 400 other children.

The law did not allow children to be removed from their parents even if the children were ill-treated or being exposed to "moral danger". Barnardo, ever the autocrat, claimed that he had a right to step in and prevent the child from being further harmed. He called this "Philanthropic Abduction". For however history judges Barnardo's intentions and motives, he himself had no doubts about their purity. He remained unaffected by frequently having to appear in the High Court, which led to demands to return children.

Much was made by Barnardo and the other philanthropists of finding the children "well-selected homes" that would be regularly inspected. The method of finding these homes, used by Barnardo and all the other charity societies, was to place ads in the local press saying that children were available and requesting replies. It was like saying a new load of produce had arrived for immediate delivery. When Barnardo opened a distribution centre in Winnipeg for ten to thirteen-year-old boys, all local farmers were notified and asked to "mention the matter to any suitable persons in your locality likely to require such help".

Children would arrive in Canada with fear and excitement, waiting to meet their Canadian family and adjust to Canadian life and work. Alex McKean remembered that:

> Dr Barnardo was at the ship to bid us farewell when my brother David and I sailed for Canada in 1905. David was nine and I was eleven . . . On our arrival in Canada we went by train to Winnipeg and spent about two weeks together in the Home. There we were told we would be separated. I remember we crawled into bed together that last night and cried with our arms around each other until we went to sleep.

Barnardo drew up a standard agreement between employer and the Home which confirmed the employer (the Canadian farmer) would undertake to receive the child for a certain period, provide him or her with food, clothing and shelter, and pay a stated sum at the end of the period to Barnardo's, which would be held in trust for the child. Kenneth Bagnell, a trenchant critic of child migration to Canada, points out in his book, *The Little Immigrants*, that there was no mention of the actual amount of money to be paid or of the needs of the child. The written agreement was to make sure that "the child is supplied with the necessities of life; that the responsibilities and authority of the Home as its guardian is duly recognised; and that the child shall be fairly and justly paid for such services as it is able and expected to render".

Having opened his first distribution Home in Toronto, Barnardo started one in Winnipeg only to find it too wild and sinful for his children. He then moved further west to Russell, on the Manitoba/Saskatchewan border. In 1887, he opened a farm there to house the young boys who worked on its vast acreage. It lasted until 1908, three years after Barnardo died, when its land was mostly sold to some ex-Barnardo boys living nearby. The winter there lasts six months and it's hard to understand how young boys coped with the farmwork, the incredibly low temperatures and the sheer loneliness of the isolated farm. The weather is stressed in the diary of Edward Struthers (Barnardo's farm manager in Russell) for 1905:

1 February: February comes in in good style, 35 degrees below zero . . .
    Numbers of the lads complaining of the cold and some laying up in the house on the very thinnest provocation. Had Parkes in office and gave him a strap for breaking a hay rack and lying about the accident . . . Preparing Thomas Wood for a situation.

9 February: Very cold a.m. −25 degrees at 9 o'c and strong wind from N.E. . . . Office very cold in fact unfit to work in . . .
    Boys not making much headway at outside work on account of low temperature and wind . . .

It was often said that the boys had a curious reserve, an almost apologetic air about them. One child migrant explained "the look" some of them had this way:

I used to wonder why so many of the boys looked so blank and stupid. Now I know that it was that "what is going to happen to me now" look. I probably looked the same, because I remember feeling that way myself. The roots were gone.

The boys had a bond with the farm animals. Barnardo himself noted that they were very kind and affectionate towards them. He interpreted this as being a substitute for the love they missed as children.

He made a number of trips to Canada between 1884 and 1904, supervising and improving his operation. Just before he died he was trying to send children off to South Africa but nothing came of it. There was already cheap labour there and there were the fears that Home children were likely to mix too freely with "the natives". His Canadian operation, however, was going successfully: there were at least 1,000 would-be employers waiting for the shiploads of children arriving – 250 on each boat. But in fact, despite all attempts to make them Canadian citizens, some twenty per cent of the children returned to live in Britain when they had worked out their apprenticeship. Many, too, joined up in the First World War as a way of getting back over the Atlantic. Apart from the cruelty with which many were treated, they felt the stigma of being Home children. Not even Barnardo could change this. Janet Plume describes her late husband's first Canadian Christmas this way:

> He hung up his stocking on Christmas Eve along with the farmer's own children and excitedly waiting for morning. While the other children were pulling toys and candy from their stockings, George found only a rotten potato in his.

Other children's experiences were no better, and the girls were particularly upset by the way they were sometimes treated, by both adults and other children. One Barnardo girl said of the farming family she was sent to:

> If they had company, they used to say, "We always let our hired girl eat with us," and that used to hurt. I'd sooner be called a maid than a hired girl. Or they would say, "Oh, she's just a Home girl." It made me feel terrible, as though you had done something degrading or wrong. The children had that same attitude: that you were *just* a Home girl.

Barnardo undoubtedly cared about his children but his equally famous contemporaries, Annie Macpherson and Maria Rye, were more concerned with other matters. Perhaps they lived on a more ethereal plain where they thought only of the child's soul – for they certainly thought little of the children as humans. Maria Rye at times seemed positively hostile to the children in her care, although Annie Macpherson was more flexible and capable of more warmth.

Maria Rye was a formidable woman, difficult to deal with and often well in advance of her time. Born in 1829, she devoted much of her early life to the rights and position of women – which took determination in Victorian society. She helped provide jobs for women, first in Britain, then overseas. This might have sparked off her interest in child migration, though she always claimed that it was Lord Shaftesbury who had influenced her. She claimed that she understood girls better than boys, indeed, she said that the migration of boys should be left to Annie Macpherson.

In 1869, when she was forty, Maria Rye took her first party of girls to Canada. Over the next few years, she often crossed the Atlantic taking children to "Our Western Home" – a previous jail and courthouse in Niagara-on-the-Lake that she had bought to become her distributing Home in Canada. The girls she brought stayed there briefly before being sent out to farms.

Like almost everything she did, Maria Rye's work in Canada began and ended in controversy. Having been persuaded that child migration was worth encouraging, she wrote to *The Times* urging support for the scheme which, she said, would remove the "gutter children" from Britain's cities to Canada and the United States. The term "guttersnipe" was promptly applied to these children, worsening the stigma they already felt. But in fact, she did not take so-called "gutter children" but children who were already under the care of the Poor Law Boards of Guardians. The first party of girls came mainly from the Board of Guardians at Kirkdale Industrial School. They saw Miss Rye's proposals as a way of saving money and eagerly handed over the children, unaware of the conditions they would have to endure.

Maria Rye also drew up apprentice agreements for the children. But these had no legal validity whatsoever and once the children lost contact with the Boards of Guardians in Britain, they were largely unprotected. Nor did Maria Rye provide any supervision – this aspect of her work produced the greatest controversy and, sometimes, she even seemed to take a perverse pride in *not* having the children supervised, claiming she had no set plans, rules or policy about supervision. She often said her most difficult task was to convince people that the Canadian men and women who came forward to take the children were substantial, orderly and well-established. So, to her, inspection of the children was unimportant.

Her many critics made the obvious point. If she did not inspect the homes, how did she know that the children were being cared for by the kind of people she claimed? Even Lord Shaftesbury, who usually supported her, was moved to say in a letter to *The Times*:

> With children of this class it is not enough merely to launch them on the sea of life. Parentless, most of them friendless, they must have someone to advise them how to improve the advantages, but still more, someone to counsel and assist them in circumstances of difficulty or temptation.

Matters came to a head after a highly critical report in 1875 by Andrew Doyle, an Inspector for the Board of Guardians (see next chapter), which effectively stopped Maria Rye's operations for two years. Doyle said damningly that he did not think that any Board of Guardians in the kingdom who knew the truth about Miss Rye's system of emigration, would sanction another child to leave. But in 1877, despite her careless policies, her refusal to inspect or supervise, and her view that the children were no longer her responsibility once off her hands, she started sending more children to Canada. It's believed that she sent some 4,000 of them before the end of the century.

Her retirement was a great relief to many people – especially the children. "Our Western Home" was transferred to the Church of England Waifs and Strays Society of London. In 1877, some six years before she died, J. J. Kelso, in a report to the Ontario government called "A Special Report on the Immigration of British Children", criticised her for mishandling the children:

> The arrangements – if there could be said to be any arrangements – for the supervision of the children after going to foster homes and situations were far from adequate. Miss Rye . . . is credited with saying that the other homes were going to an unnecessary expense in maintaining a staff of visitors . . .
> The consequent danger is that the child soon realises the lack of interest that is manifested in its welfare: and the foster parents see they are not likely to be interfered with if they overwork and otherwise take advantage of their young charges.

Maria Rye's contemporary, Annie Macpherson, escaped such criticism, she was more adaptable. She was born in 1833 and educated in Glasgow. Always serious, in 1859 she had a profound religious experience which, like Barnardo, transformed her into a devout evangelical. She moved to London in 1862 and became caught up in the plight of children in the East End. Her book, *The Little Matchbox Makers,* describes the virtual slavery of those children who were expected to make a gross of matchboxes for just three farthings. She became convinced that the only answer was emigration.

Annie Macpherson had three Homes in Canada. "Marchmont" opened in 1870 and took children from various Homes in Britain: from "The Refuge" and "Home of Industry" in London; from "The Manchester Boys and Girls' Refuge"; from the "Canadian Emigration Home" in Bristol; and "The Saltcoats Orphanage" in Glasgow. The second Home was opened near Galt, Ontario, in 1871 and the third in Knowlton, Quebec, the following year.

Annie Macpherson, unlike Maria Rye, did at least try to supervise the children, and was praised by Andrew Doyle as being "a true and disinterested benefactor". She recognised some of the faults in her approach and, after the Doyle report, tried to remedy them. For example, Andrew Doyle had objected to mixing workhouse children with the waifs and strays, so Annie Macpherson refused to take out any more workhouse children. And once the risks of taking out grown girls as domestic servants had been pointed out to her, she only took very young children – not that this was much of an improvement!

She retained strong links with Barnardo, so it was no accident that her organisation was taken over by Barnardo on her retirement. She was popular and respected, both in Britain and Canada, deeply committed to the cause of child migration and has been called the most efficient and benign of the philanthropists. The people she employed to run her homes were of sound judgement and were kind. But still she failed to understand the effects on the children.

It is easy to see Barnardo, Annie Macpherson and Maria Rye as dominating the scene. Yet philanthropists all over Britain were involved. In Scotland, the most important figure was William Quarrier, an evangelical child-saver who ran the Orphan Home of Scotland and a farm school at Bridge of Weir. He began his public work in 1864 in Glasgow and opened his first Home there in 1871. The same year he began to take parties of children to Canada, distributing them through Annie Mapherson's Marchmont Home in Belleville, Ontario. In 1888 he established his own receiving Home, "Fairknowe", in Brockville, Ontario. Like Annie Macpherson but unlike Barnardo, Quarrier insisted the guardians of the child gave their consent before the child could enter his Home.

The organisation aimed at caring for the fatherless and destitute children of Scotland; any such child in any part of Scotland was eligible for admission. Their friends were exhorted to apply on behalf of the child and "thus help save the little ones from want and misery".

Reports on the Canadian distribution Home for the Quarrier children say it was "well run with a decent class of boys and girls".

Quarrier was convinced of the success of this branch of his work. In 1888, after seventeen years' involvement with child migration and having taken about 3,000 children to Canada, he claimed that ninety-five per cent of the children were doing well – though he didn't expand on what he meant. Quarrier contrasted this happy state of affairs to the position back home, where such children were affected "by the dragging-down influences of their relations and whole surroundings". At one church service, after the child migrants left the Quarrier Home at the Bridge of Weir, those remaining sang:

> Don't forget the Orphan Homes of Scotland,
> Don't forget the dear friends here;
> Don't forget that Jesus Christ, your Saviour
> Goes with thee to Canada.
>
> And remember we are still a-praying
> That your life will be good and true,
> And that you may find a blessing
> In the land you are going to.

The Quarriers, William and his wife, often went to Canada and tried as best they could to inspect all the children. But it was a hopeless task: with 3,000 children placed by 1888, what chance was there of adequate inspection? In one visit, lasting three months, they saw 300 children and received reports on a great many more, though these were less valuable. Even so, the claims for success were great: "It would be difficult," said William Quarrier, in a report he wrote in 1888, "to describe the comfortable homes and favourable circumstances in which we found the children . . . To some of them the happy family life was a thing unknown before . . ."

These annual reports always contained glowing testimonies to the success of the Canadian venture, as an example from the 1888 report shows:

Little L was a picture of neatness – white stockings and dainty little boots. Quite a pet.

J has been in one place till this summer, when he wished to learn a trade, so has gone to Toronto. Mr M said he would not hinder him for he had done his duty by him and would no doubt be faithful wherever placed.

This is the best boy you ever sent out. I have had him nine years and I know no difference between him and my own.

Only once, in a 1916 report, was there a veiled hint that the scheme was perhaps less successful, and this was quickly turned to advantage:

> Much additional work resulted from the restlessness of many boys on account of their desire to join the Army at much too early an age ... Probably no Canadian Regiment has crossed the ocean in the past two years without having some four boys in its ranks.

However, despite all their plans to extend their work, the Quarrier Homes, and their emigration work in Canada, faded away in 1925 and they, like others, had to turn their attention to Australia.

The Roman Catholic Church also sent children to Canada but only one Catholic society was involved at the turn of the century: the South Catholic Emigration Society, founded by the Bishop of Southwark in London. The society had begun sending children to Canada in 1882. Those from the dioceses of Westminster, Southwark, Birmingham and Liverpool were originally sent to the province of Quebec but, because of the difficulties of placing boys in English-speaking homes there, the society opened a boys' Home called New Orpington Lodge in Hintonburg, Ontario (now a part of Ottawa) in 1896. The name was later changed to the St George's Home and it was run by the Sisters of the English Order of St Paul the Apostle. The society continued placing girls in Quebec through the St Anne's Home in Montreal; it also had a farm in Mackinac, Ontario.

Although the Roman Catholic organisations were comparatively late in entering the child migration stakes, once they started, they stayed on ruthlessly right to the end. It was mainly the Catholics' rivalry with Barnardo and their fear of his Protestant fervour – he was known to dislike Catholicism – that spurred them into action. The Catholic Church suspected that Barnardo was taking Catholic children and placing them in Protestant homes, thereby converting them to Protestantism. The idea horrified them and they decided they had to stop this. But how? They couldn't afford to build enough Homes and orphanages to house the numbers placed with them. Emigration was the answer if the faith was to be preserved, and so determined were they to defend their faith, that they even placed children with non-English speaking French-Canadian families, devoted to their religion. They simply ignored the effect on the children who were faced with not only having to survive in a strange country but also having to learn a new language. It was a sad reprise of the time English children were placed with Afrikaans in South Africa, a century or so earlier. The history of the Catholic societies in Australia, after Canada, is another chapter in the history of child migration. It is not a chapter of which they can be wholly proud.

The lists of societies and organisations involved in child migration at the end of the nineteenth century is extremely long and all the different churches were represented. One dominant figure, Kingsley Fairbridge of the Fairbridge Scheme, is described in all his empire-building glory in Chapter 6. Some societies used the distributing centres of major organisations like Barnardo's, while others had their own. Even those which "borrowed" distribution centres might keep control over placing the children and inspecting them, others relinquished it completely.

The Church of England Waifs and Strays Society (later the Church of England's Children's Society) was one of the large societies involved which had its own special administrative framework. The society, initially called the Church of England Incorporated Society for providing Homes for Waifs and Strays, was founded in 1881. In 1884, it began to send boys to Canada, to a home in Sherbrooke, Quebec, operated and run on its behalf. In 1896, the society took over Maria Rye's "Our Western Home" and it became the society's distribution Home for girls, who were then sent to Church of England families. It was taken over by the army in the First World War and never reopened. In 1924, it opened the Elizabeth Rye Home in Toronto, for girls of between fourteen to eighteen, destined to be domestic servants, but the Home got so many complaints about the morality and mental ability of these girls that it closed in 1931. The society then moved on to Australia.

Founded by Dr T. B. Stephenson in 1869, the National Children's Home and Orphanage sent its first party of forty-nine boys and girls to Canada in 1873, "to take advantage of the ampler opportunities of colonial life". It included Jack ("a wild, rough lad"), Harry ("who had given so much trouble in the past") and Marian ("the daughter of a drunken London crossing sweeper"). A Home was established at Hamilton, Ontario, with eight acres of land, and over 3,000 children were sent out before the 1920s and its closure.

The Salvation Army and the Methodists were also involved. The Salvation Army sent a number of children to Canada, but although they had to be aged between fourteen and eighteen and were all sent on a course of instruction (such duties as stable work, land work, carpentry and cooking and household duties) many slipped through the net. The Boys' and Girls' Refuges (now known as the Boys' and Girls' Welfare Society) sent over 2,000 children to Canada between 1871 and 1915, to a distribution Home. From here they were sent out to farms.

The Wesleyan Methodist National Children's Homes, in England, headed by Dr Thomas Bowman, had orphanages and Homes in Kent, Warwickshire, the Isle of Man and Hampshire. Bowman started to send children to his receiving Home in Hamilton, Ontario, in 1872 and from then on about 250 a year went out. At first both boys and girls were sent, but then boys only. James W. C. Fegan, who founded a number of Homes and orphanages in Deptford, London, sent boys to Canada from 1872 to 1903. He began sending boys, mostly aged sixteen or seventeen, to his distributing Home in Toronto in 1884. From the Toronto Home they were placed locally on farms but, unlike children from many other schemes, Fegan's children were older and could look after themselves – except that having been living on the streets of London for years they had a difficult time settling down to the monotony of farm life. A weakness in Fegan's scheme, and this applied to other philanthropists as well, was that the boys spent too little time in orphanages in London before leaving for Canada (some as little as a day or two). Hardly surprising, then, that they had too little time to learn what were described as "better attitudes".

In 1872, the same year as Fegan, John Middlemore opened the Children's Emigrants Home in Birmingham, followed by a Home for girls. The Home's records say, "Emigration is the only mode of permanently separating these children from their old associations." In fact, Middlemore claimed that the parent was always considered before a child was "removed" to an emigration Home. From here they went to "Fairview", his own receiving Home for boys and girls, in Halifax, Nova Scotia and children were then distributed around Nova Scotia, New Brunswick and Prince Edward Island. "Fairview" was a Protestant non-denominational Home.

The Middlemore Homes, which eventually amalgamated with the Fairbridge Farms, had a poor reputation. There were serious doubts about how much care was used to select farms for the children – though one form of agreement between an employer and the Fairview Home read caringly enough:

> I promise to take and adopt Henry Jones and to treat him in all respects as if he were my own child: to attend to and supply, as far as I can, all his needs, to send him to school and to church or to chapel: and finally to teach him, or cause him to be taught, some trade or calling, by attention to which he may make himself an honourable and independent position.

If the agreement had always been held to, perhaps the children's dreams on that ship might have come true. But as so often with these agreements, the reality was different. One newspaper report on three children who were sent out through Middlemore in 1911, for instance, described how they "were forced into a routine of relentless work which included endless barn chores and house-work".

> If that wasn't bad enough, they were made to go in their bare feet from Spring to Fall. Sometimes it was so cold that they would make the cows get up from lying down so they could put their feet there to get them warm.

These children were tearfully separated on arrival – the younger brother being sent to a farm eighteen kilometres away and not seen by the others for ten years. Commenting on this, one seventy-four-year-old woman, who went out in 1928 said:

> That was typical. They would only be just a few miles from each other and they just never let you know. It must have been deliberate, so we couldn't get in touch with each other.

Indeed, the Middlemore director once seriously argued that he did not think the work of bringing child immigrants to Canada should be under the Director of Child Welfare but under *the Department of Natural Resources*. Not surprisingly the plight of these children was often desperate and their welfare disregarded by those who were responsible for them. This account by John Middlemore of his first venture shows staggering irresponsi-bility:

> I left for Canada with twenty-nine children on the 1st May 1893. The journey was entirely one of discovery and speculation. I had not a single friend in Canada and did not know what to do with the children when I arrived there. In the course of my enquiries I heard of the Hon. George Allen and Professor D. Wilson of Toronto, and sent them telegrams soliciting help. Both these gentlemen interfered most gener-ously and most cordially on my behalf. They procured temporary lodgings for my children and treated me with much personal kindness. My arrival was made known by articles in the Toronto newspaper and by personal correspondence, and in the course of three or four weeks I had found good homes for all my children.

No one queried the assumptions behind his comments about Canada, Britain, the relationship between them, the way homes were provided for the children and what kind of Canadian farmers were providing them.

There were also many Homes and boys' "clubs" based on a particular city or town that sent their own children off to the other side of the world, such as the Nottingham Dakeyne Street Club, founded in 1909 by a local solicitor, Mr Oliver Hind. In 1913, the Dakeyne Street Boys' Farm was opened in Nova Scotia so that Dakeyne Street Club lads could emigrate to Canada under "safe" conditions. By 1930 about 200 boys had passed through the farm. It took older children – the club's old boys – and was said to be a "complete success in both individual settlement and in real Empire building". Like so many of the charities' own reports on their operations, it sounds as if the children were well cared for. But, as was so often the case, when you hear the accounts of the child migrants themselves, first hand, the full story of hardship and exploitation emerges (see Charles Devonport's story, Chapter 2).

There was also an organisation in Glasgow, run by Dr G. C. Cossar, which sent boys to New Brunswick. Others were: the Coombe Homes in Dublin, which used Annie Macpherson's organisations to distribute its children; the Shaftesbury Home, which used the Barnardo organisation to bring the children to Canada but then dealt with the children itself through its Winnipeg distribution centre; and the Bristol Emigration Society, managed by Mrs M. E. Forster, which sent children to Canada unaccompanied even by a guardian.

All the organisations concerned with child migration differed in quality, methods and philosophy – though, for the children, the end result was still exploitation and cheap labour. It is hard to gauge just how many were sent overseas during this philanthropic phase, as there were few records. Estimates vary from 80,000 to 100,000: in 1988 the Canadian Government Archives Division put the figure at 90,000.

Child migration was seen as a safety-valve against unemployment. It was seriously suggested that unemployed pauper children were likely to become a discontented underclass, threatening the stability of British society. Some verses from the poem "The Departure of the Innocents" sum up the nineteenth-century attitude:

> Take them away! Take them away!
> Out of the gutter, the ooze, and slime,
> Where the little vermin paddle and crawl
> Till they grow and ripen into crime.
>
> Take them away! Take them away!
> The boys from the gallows, the girls from worse;
> They'll prove a blessing to other lands –
> Here, if they linger, they'll prove a curse.

Take them away! Take them away!
To con the lesson they never knew,
And can never learn mid the reek and rot
Of the sweltering garbage where they grew:

The lesson that work is the gift of Heaven –
A blessing to lighten all human ill,
And that the generous earth affords
Work and Reward to all who will.

Take them away! Away! Away!
The bountiful earth is wide and free,
The New shall repair the wrongs of the Old –
God be with them over the sea!

Those who praise the philanthropists ignore one brutal fact: the children invariably didn't want to go. Time and again, in talking to these migrants, the same words are used, "They gave me the choice between Canada and Australia." Just the choice of which country – and many didn't even have that – *not* the choice of whether they would like to go at all. Of course, children often put up their hands to go, with absolutely no idea at the age of seven, eight or nine, what it entailed – it sounded like a nice day trip. Some older children, aged eleven or twelve, were keen to leave unhappy surroundings in Britain, perhaps a parent remarrying who didn't want them around, grandparents who couldn't cope or a Home they were unhappy in. But the children – whether sent in the 1880s or 1960s – were cut off from their family and roots and were far too young to have any inclination towards farming or service in Canada, Australia or Rhodesia. As one child migrant, who was twelve when he left Durham for the Fairbridge Farm School in Pinjarra, said:

They tore you out of where you belong. That's what gets you. It hurts you.

Another, who went to Australia at the age of eleven, agreed:

It was deeply traumatic for me as it was for most of the children. I think now, looking back, the whole idea of it worries me. They were taking children away, often from their parents, and just putting them out of the way.

It is a damning indictment of the philanthropists.

5

The Breakdown of Philanthropy

The child migration movement increased in intensity under the philanthropists, despite the damning evidence of the Doyle Report. This government inquiry into child migration sharply painted the miseries in store for the children and concluded forcefully that child migration was *wrong*. Its criticisms and solutions were constantly ignored for the next one hundred years.

Andrew Doyle was an unlikely contender for such a controversial report. Already sixty-five when he began his investigations, he had been trained as a barrister but spent his life working as a civil servant on the Poor Law. He was known to prefer workhouse education and training to the "boarding out" (foster care) system.

Doyle was asked by the Local Government Board to follow up and inspect children sent to Canada at the ratepayers' expense, in 1874. Earlier that year a number of complaints had been made about the Canadian system: some of the girls had become pregnant and there were allegations of ill-treatment of some of the children in Canada. This sometimes took place while the children were still in the care of the voluntary societies responsible for them, before they were even placed with farm families.

The report directly concerns Maria Rye and Annie Macpherson because they took children to Canada through the Poor Law Board of Guardians. In 1870, the Poor Law Board had sanctioned the emigration of pauper children to Canada under these two women's care. Its annual report that year urged the Boards of Guardians "to avail themselves of the means which the active benevolence of Miss Rye and Miss Macpherson has provided for the welfare of the children who are sent out as emigrants".

Andrew Doyle's brief covered the way the children were collected in Britain, their selection for Canada, the receiving Homes in Canada, the way they were selected for farmers in Canada and, particularly, the inspection and follow-up care of these children. He spent six months, from June to October 1874, collecting information, travelling around Canada and visiting children. It was no easy task for a man of his age and habits and he found it hard and laborious. Altogether, he saw about 400 children, spent time in Montreal where most of the children entered Canada and spoke to immigration officials, agents and officers. He toured the receiving Homes and he talked to Annie Macpherson and Maria Rye and their assistants. He examined the children's records and saw how they were treated in the Homes. He was particularly concerned about those unsuitable for farm life and who were returned as unsuitable. But above all he saw the children themselves and the work they did on the farms.

Andrew Doyle's report was completed in January 1875 and published on 8 February 1875. His flat civil service prose heightened its dramatic details and the reactions were immediate. A retiring figure, he was suddenly at the centre of public controversy, clashing spectacularly with Maria Rye. The two of them couldn't have been more different. Doyle attacked the very philosophy of child migration, saying that as every Board of Guardians in the United Kingdom had the means to train pauper children for jobs, especially those in domestic service, why send them to Canada? He gave the answer himself: to provide cheap labour. He threw some accolades to the two women but effectively the report damned both women (though particularly Maria Rye), criticising all their methods from the time the children were sent to Canada to the point where they were placed on Canadian farms.

Take, first, the way the children were found and selected for Canada.

> Miss Rye has a "Home" at Peckham, into which she received "waifs" and "strays", professing to train them for emigration to Canada . . . Miss Mapherson has informed me that she makes no application to Boards of Guardians to commit pauper children to her care, that the applications come from the Guardians to her. Miss Rye, upon the other hand, makes her scheme known by circular letters, in which she explains the conditions under which the girls are put out to service, and undertakes that they shall "be looked after until they are eighteen years of age . . ."
>
> In the cases of infants, and of orphans or deserted children of the [street] "arab" class, it is alleged that the authority of the legal guardian is obtained. This, I apprehend, will be found to be done in a very loose and informal way.

He was quick to see through the lofty language of the child exporters:

> Miss Macpherson desired it to be understood that her work is and always has been essentially, if not exclusively, of a missionary

character . . . in reality it is an agency for the promotion of emigration involving schemes for providing cheap labour for Canadian farmers.

Doyle found that the way the children were collected for their journey to Canada worked like this. As soon as Miss Macpherson or Miss Rye collected a large enough party of children, about one hundred to 200, notice of the day of sailing from Liverpool was given to all Homes. Children from London were brought by Miss Rye or Miss Macpherson; those from elsewhere came in the charge of the Master of the local Poor Law workhouse, who delivered them to either of the women. Sometimes these Masters stayed with the children until the ship sailed, sometimes they didn't.

When he himself sailed to Canada with 150 children aged between six and fourteen years, in Miss Rye's charge, Doyle's main concern was that they were brought out in such large numbers. He also felt one supervisor was far from enough, especially with the close quarters of the arrangements and the frequent seasickness.

> Such an arrangement is the more necessary, as the personal cleanliness of the children is very much neglected during the voyage. Upon their arrival at the Homes a very considerable number of them are found to be in a most filthy condition, their heads swarming with vermin.

"We all sicked over each other," one boy told him. And Miss Macpherson, describing to him her first passage out with a hundred boys, admitted to "nearly all the lads being very seasick" and that, "They lay like herrings in a barrel around the funnel on deck, in nooks under the small boats; some too bad to be hauled up the ladder. No small work was it to cheer and rouse them out of this condition."

After arrival in Canada, Doyle noted that Miss Macpherson's children broke their journey to Ontario at St George's Home, Montreal, "of which all I can say is, that under its present management, the shorter the time children are allowed to remain in it the better". Of Miss Rye's many children, Doyle said, "For so large a number the offices, washing accommodation, etc, would fall short of the official requirements of an ordinary English workhouse."

He was concerned about the fact that there was no way of isolating any children with infectious diseases, even though one of the Homes at Knowlton had recently had an outbreak of scarlet fever, and one child had been returned to a Home suffering from typhoid. He was also dismayed by what some of the children told him about their treatment while in one or other of the Homes:

> One intelligent girl complained that "the bread was mouldy, and what
> was called meat was unfit to eat". Another, to whose truthfulness her
> mistress testified somewhat emphatically by saying, "You couldn't
> hire that girl to tell a lie," described to me her punishment at "Our
> Western Home" for having been returned for bad temper, or, as I find
> it recorded by Miss Rye, "violent temper". She was placed in a room
> at the top of the house (it is a large airy room) and kept there in
> solitary confinement for eleven days upon bread and water, without
> book or work to divert her thoughts.

Doyle's reaction was sharp: "Should not some prescribed
regulations put it out of the power of any irresponsible person to
do so grievous a wrong to a child for any offence whatever?" On
hearing that the managers of the Homes encouraged the children
to look on the Homes as places of refuge "in any time of trouble or
distress", he said:

> I cannot say that I think they have been successful in creating such a
> feeling of confidence. Over and over again I have been told of the
> dread of children to go back to the Home, and employers have
> observed to me that as a last resource, when all other means had failed,
> they had to "threaten to send them back to the Home".

He came across one girl who had called at the Home after
leaving several employers and was handed advice rather than
practical help. She became pregnant and Doyle asked her to call in
at the Home, only to receive this letter:

> Dear Sir, I write to tell you that I would very much like to see you on
> Wednesday, but no, I cannot any more have the heart to go to
> Marchmont [the Home], for it has never been a home for me, although
> it was told to me and all the rest, that when we came to Canada it was
> to be a home. But, sir, I have known the time when I would have been
> glad for a bit to eat and a bed to lie on, for I my own self have had to
> sleep in barns for a shelter when the snow have been so thick, and no
> person would be seen out, and have been to Marchmont for a shelter,
> and was turned away, so that I have nothing to thank them for . . . as
> long as they can bring out poor children to be pounded half to death,
> and slave to the uttermost, that is all they care for.

Doyle also noted that the method of placing children was
extremely unsatisfactory:

> Owing to the very rapid dispersion of these young emigrants, the
> sending them into service immediately upon their arrival in Canada,
> Miss Rye or Miss Macpherson, or their representatives, can know very

little – in the majority of pauper cases absolutely nothing – of their character or disposition, or peculiar aptitude, if they have any, or unfitness for service. Yet the success of a child will very often depend upon its finding a suitable first place . . .

When one thinks what must be the depressing effect upon a child of being sent back to the Home disappointed and discouraged by early failure, it is impossible not to feel very strongly that those who assume the responsibility of finding homes for them should have patience – keeping the children, notwithstanding the additional expense, until they could learn something of their tempers, dispositions, and fitness for service, and something too of the temper and disposition of the people to whom they send them, so that there might be a reasonable chance of employer and child getting on together.

Miss Macpherson usually sent out a notification of the kind of children available before they arrived. Applicants had to send a letter of recommendation from their minister and from a respectable resident. Upon receipt the request was usually granted and an agreement made. Miss Rye used a different method. When applicants wrote in for a child, they were asked to give particulars of themselves. If satisfactory, the children were sent out, usually through private people in different districts. Doyle's dry comment on this was:

Miss Rye trusts to the accident of being able to find persons in different districts who will relieve her from the responsibility not only of finding suitable homes but of looking after the children when they are placed in them.

He visited one couple who did this on her behalf, and said:

The duty that is voluntarily undertaken by Mr and Mrs Robson appears to be admirably discharged. In some other districts, however, Miss Rye does not appear to have been equally fortunate . . . The persons who place the children out are often either misled or very imperfectly informed as to the character of applicants for children . . .

Had all the homes been "selected by persons who have an intimate knowledge of the locality", children would not have been placed in such homes as those in which I found some of them, nor if strict inquiry had been made both as to the requirements and character of applicants for children should we hear of such cases as a child being brought back, because it was "too small", then sent to another place "next day", then brought back, "because the man drank"; a second brought back "because he was with rough men and learning to swear"; another – several others – for being "too small", as if that could not have been seen before the children were placed out, another because "his master drank"; several changed because "people were not kind to them . . ."

Doyle's experiences convinced him that any system that allowed
children to be placed in homes about which little or nothing was
known by the philanthropic agencies, with hardly any supervision,
was wrong. When he was travelling through Ontario and Quebec,
he found "intolerable evidence of ill treatment, overwork and
physical abuse", and wanted to set up a formal system to place the
children, not one run by well-meaning volunteers. He also criticised the "legal" agreements or indentures made over the child's
head between the Home and their would-be Canadian employer.

> For the disposal of a large proportion of the girls, both Miss
> Macpherson and Miss Rye depend upon what they term "adoption".
> In the system of each this word has two distinct meanings. Very young
> children are "adopted" in the ordinary sense of the word . . . The other
> sense in which the word "adoption" is used is simply appren-
> ticeship . . . The view that many of the children take of this form of
> "adoption" was expressed to me by one of them, an intelligent shrewd
> girl of between sixteen and seventeen. "'Doption, sir, is when folks
> gets a girl to work without wages." The whole of this machinery of
> "indentures", though it has a look of being business-like, appears to
> me to be worthless or delusive . . . No one can wonder at the
> restlessness and dissatisfaction of boys and girls of fifteen and sixteen
> who find themselves "adopted", that is bound to serve without wages,
> merely for their maintenance and clothing, until they are eighteen.

The indentures were worthless because they offered no immediate security for the children and little future protection. They also
tied children to the farmer until they were aged eighteen.

> I cannot help thinking that in a country in which wages are so high and
> the cost of living for a child at least so low that terms of service are for
> the children less favourable than they ought to be.

These agreements did not mention the need to have these
children inspected, so there was no check whatsoever on whether
the conditions of adoption had been fulfilled. Doyle also disliked
the way all children were under the "parental control" of both
women.

> Whether children who are brought to Canada have been legally placed
> under the care of the persons who bring them is a point left wholly
> unnoticed by the authorities of the Dominion or of the Provinces.

One result of this was that some children, originally sent to
Canada, ended up by being placed in the United States. This was
not only contrary to the conditions under which they were
entrusted to a guardian's care (the guardian was Miss Rye), but

it broke the rules of the government department that had originally sanctioned their emigration to Canada. The number of those who went to the States was relatively small (only forty-six by 1894) but Miss Rye admitted that "others had been known to go". And it shows how easy it was to send the children across the border.

It also shows the callous disregard for the legal rights of the children, who were regarded as so much farm-fodder. Legal consent had to be obtained from either a legal guardian (for street arabs) or the Board of Guardians (for paupers) but Doyle had already found that this was done "loosely". One of his observations, which surfaces time and again throughout the history of child migration right up until the last shiploads of children to Australia in the late 1960s, was this one:

> I met with several cases of children sent out as orphans who had one if not both parents living.

Doyle travelled extensively around Canada to see how the children placed with Canadian families were getting on:

> I have several times driven through miles of forests to find the child of whom I was in quest in a remote log hut, or "shanty", the settler's first home, just put up upon the few acres of recently cleared land.

He makes a fundamental point about the nature of the jobs given to these children:

> It is taking a favourable view of the position of a servant-of-all-work in the house of a small tradesman, or of a nurse girl in the family of a mechanic, to say that it is no better in Canada than it is in England. Some of the places indeed are worse than a Board of Guardians would consent to place a child in England.

Again, this is a point that comes up constantly. Were these children really better off being sent abroad? Some undoubtedly were, but what about all those that were not? Hundreds of advertisements were put out by organisations and societies involved in child migration, begging for money to give children a better life in the new world. On paper, it sounded inspiring: the reality was often tragically different.

Doyle was particularly angry about the lack of inspection. Several employers complained to him that no one seemed to take an interest in the children after they were placed – no one visited them or inquired about them. Although he met few cases of gross cruelty, he discovered many cases of ill-treatment and hardship. As Miss Rye boasted of having "no set plans, no rules, no sharply defined policy about overlooking the children in Canada", this is hardly surprising. In one instance a girl called Mary Ford had been sent to Miss Rye in 1873 by the Guardians of Merthyr Tydfil and subsequently placed in service with a family in Hamilton, Ontario. On asking for her in the street where he knew she lived, Doyle was told by a neighbour:

> Oh, I am glad anybody has come to look after her. I have seen that child flogged worse than a slave, but don't mention me as telling you, for I do all the white washing of the house.

When Doyle questioned the girl's mistress, she told him the girl had a bad character and that she had written more than once to Miss Rye asking for her to be taken away but had received no reply. Doyle lists other examples of ill-treatment:

> A girl complained to me that "for temper" she had been sent to bed on Saturday afternoon and kept there without food till Sunday evening; a mistress told me that she had kept a girl on bread and water for three days for refusing to admit that she had stolen five cents; a master I ascertained had horse-whipped a girl of thirteen; I found the marks of a flogging on a boy's shoulders, the flogging having been inflicted a fortnight before: in reply to my question, "Why did you leave your former place?" the answer would very often be to the effect, if not in so many words, "I couldn't manage to please them, they were always scolding me, they used to beat me, I was very unhappy." The number of such cases that are unnoticed because not visited are, I fear, very considerable.

Many societies and organisations concerned with child migration point proudly to their records, which show that they had inspectors who sent back some pretty glowing reports. But these reports are totally suspect: many child migrants say that they were sent out of the way when an inspector came to call. Doyle himself pointed out discrepancies between the inspector's report and the truth. Take the case of the girl who told him that she had received "a pitiable letter" from her brother, saying he had been sent to a farmer who "used him very badly". The girl's employer got the boy back and managed to get him another job with a saw maker, who twice turned him out of doors. On the last occasion he was found at the corner of the street sitting on his box crying. Doyle says that:

> The information furnished to the Guardians about him from Canada is: "Good accounts are received from this child. He is at St. Catherine's, in a gentleman's family." The boy's own description of the place in "a gentleman's family" was that his master was a "sort of middlin'

farmer"; that he was put to wash the dishes, scrub floors, drive cattle, and do little chores about the house. The good woman who so kindly interested herself for the boy observed to me – "You are the first person, sir, who has ever been to visit these children or to make any inquiry about them."

Doyle accepted that the Canadian farmer worked hard himself but he insisted that inspections should be carried out, particularly with children who were put to work at an extremely early age, and that extra staff should be taken on. Given what happened to many of the children sent over, it is almost unbelievable that Doyle should find an item in Miss Macpherson's accounts called "Repayment of Passage Money".

Miss Macpherson has been in the habit of inviting children to repay the cost of their emigration in order to assist the emigration of other children. This has always been carefully explained to the children, but even with such explanation, I think it is a mistake to allow a child to contribute £6 or £7 nominally as repayment of passage money.

In fact, although the philanthropists involved in child migration piously claimed that they were above tawdry concerns about money and profits, not only was the one-off cost of sending a child overseas cheaper than years of looking after it in Britain but Doyle made another discovery. After looking at the books of both of their organisations he concluded "that the receipts upon account of pauper immigrants in 1873 and 1874 would very considerably exceed the expenditure". He was able to show that there was about a one hundred per cent profit on each transaction. The Poor Law Guardians in Britain paid out £8 a child (as well as a full outfit of clothing) and the Ontario government added £1. 4s. 6d. The cost of the passage from Liverpool to the distributing Home in Toronto was £3. 15s. and the assumed cost for each child at the Home was £1. This left a profit on each child of £4. 9s. Doyle accused them of "not being wholly actuated by motives of benevolence".

Not all of his report is critical. The diet of the children in the Homes was, on the whole, "good and sufficient"; the very young children who were genuinely adopted, rather than being put into service, "are usually treated with kindness, becoming practically members of the family". He also said that it was "impossible to speak too highly" of what Miss Macpherson and Miss Rye were endeavouring to do for the "street arabs".

He drew a sharp line between the street arabs ("of the very lowest classes – the semi-criminals of our large cities and towns") and the pauper (workhouse) children, whose emigration was sanctioned by the Boards of Guardians and who, unlike the "arabs" mostly had at least a few years of education. He thought it disgraceful that these two groups were mixed, so that the poor reputation of the street kids was spreading to the paupers and this was not "favourable to future success". It was hardly the fault of the street kids: they had received no training whatsoever and were faced with the appalling task of readjusting from hanging about on city streets to doing menial work on isolated Canadian farms.

Doyle thought that before both types of children were placed in Canada, they should be given a long period of training, preferably in Canada itself, and that the two groups should remain separate until the street kids were on a level with the paupers. He also said forcefully that no girls over eight should be sent out as those aged from nine to fifteen were immediately placed in service.

> By whatever name that service may be called, though disguised as "adoption", it is in fact domestic service, quite as hard as, and in some respects more uninviting to the children, than the service in which at the same age they might be placed out in England.

Doyle succeeded in revealing the ruthless exploitation of the children. It was his view that British children ought to expect elementary safeguards wherever they were and his report aimed at providing them. Few others shared his views, either then or later. Maria Rye certainly didn't. Stung by the accusations against her, including the one which said she made a profit on each migrant child, she in turn attacked Andrew Doyle and against all odds, expectations or rational thinking, she won the day. She did so by conjuring up support from wealthy, important Canadian figures who supported child migration. Naturally enough, their support was entirely selfish for Canada's economic and agricultural development was progressing fast and child migration was an important factor. In the "Report of the Proceedings of the Committee of the House of Commons on Immigration and Colonialisation", held on 10 March 1875 in Canada, supporters of child migration came out in force. They recognised that if Doyle's report was accepted, it would put a stop to child migration altogether. The time had come to defend it, and defend it they did.

Some members of the Canadian Committee accused the Doyle report of being "erroneous in its conclusions". They claimed they had personal knowledge of the work done by Miss Rye and Miss Macpherson and it was "highly advantageous to all concerned". (Presumably the children didn't count.) One supporter said Doyle's proposal for making the reception Homes in Canada into training centres would extend the British workhouse system to

Canada. That, he said, would be unsatisfactory and unsuitable to Canadian conditions. Another criticised Doyle for being "prejudiced against the charitable work being undertaken". And another said he was astonished that anyone could so persistently present the dark side of the picture. It seemed that Doyle would merely establish "red-tapeism" as all the children would have to be inspected by government employees. Accusations like this stoked traditional Canadian fears of central government control and bureaucratic intervention, and acted as body blows to Doyle's hopes of Canadian support for his recommendations.

Miss Macpherson and Miss Rye also appeared before the Immigration and Colonialisation Committee and produced testimony that their work was a success. They pointed out that they were currently bringing out children to Canada at the rate of about 400 or 500 a year: Miss Macpherson had brought out about 2,000 (1,700 boys, 300 girls) between 1870 and 1875; Miss Rye had brought about 1,000 (mainly girls) between 1867 and 1869. Their figures showed that only about 350 of the 2,000 were taken from workhouses.

Both women claimed their efforts had met with every success and that only about one per cent of the children were "failures". They said that they only got about £2 a head from the Canadian government – less than that stated by Doyle. And they produced testimonials by influential Church figures, supporting their efforts. Take the one from the Lord Bishop of Toronto in support of Miss Rye:

Toronto, March 29, 1875

My Dear Miss Rye,
    I am sincerely grieved for the trouble you are experiencing as indicated in your letter of the 25th from Ottawa.
    I have all along considered your work a boon to Canada: and although disappointments are inevitable the general success of your enterprise has surprised and satisfied us all.
    I have on more than one occasion been present at happy gatherings of your young people: but on no more gratifying one than on the 22nd September last when as I understand nearly 300 were present with those whom we may call foster parents.
    I have met several of your girls at friends' houses in the country and with very few exceptions received a good account of them. From all I heard they were in great demand: and any check to your benevolent enterprise through calumny or misapprehension would be a wide felt disappointment.

Believe me dear Miss Rye
Very Sincerely Yours
[Signed] A. H. Toronto

Armed with testimonials like this, the two could not fail. But there was one final damning condemnation of Doyle yet to come. Andrew Doyle was a Roman Catholic. There was no way, with a slur like that against him, that he could fight against two such righteous Protestant ladies – particularly given the hostility between the two religions. Being a Catholic, Doyle was naturally bound to be motivated by malice and envy – there was the explanation for the things he said. His bias was unmasked, his evils made clear, his mistakes understood and his attacks placed in perspective. And so Andrew Doyle was discredited and his report ultimately banished to oblivion. Another twenty-five years would pass before his views were even given consideration.

For the two years after the Doyle Report, 1875 to 1877, child migration declined but little effort was made to look at alternative ways of helping destitute children. There was such a way but it was much less popular than child migration because it was more expensive, more time-consuming and more difficult to adminster. It was called Boarding Out and was similar to our current system of fostering, whereby destitute children were placed with families. Stringent regulations governed boarding out in England and Scotland. It's unfortunate that the same protection shown to British children who were boarding out wasn't extended to the child migrants. After the drop in numbers following the Doyle Report, they then actually increased. Barnardo began transporting children overseas about seven years after the report and then went to sending about 1,000 children a year. Others did the same and immigration spiralled. In the five years between 1883 and 1889 nearly 2,000 children a year were sent to Canada. The immense demand for them is shown in a letter written in Canada in June 1884 by a labourer's wife, who took over two girls of over twelve and one boy and three girls of under twelve. After writing that she has successfully placed the three eldest girls, she continues:

> There has been lots of ladies after my other two little girls that have not got any children of their own, but I don't know what I shall do about that yet. If I had brought a hundred girls and boys out with me, I could get good places for them all. The folks here are crazy after English children.

Not all Doyle's recommendations were ignored however. For example, pre-sailing physical examinations began in 1888 after complaints in the Canadian Parliament about the children's health, and stricter attention was paid to the children's health before landing. The reason for this was not concern for the children – just fear of them spreading disease in Canada. But generally child migration was boosted by romantic dreams of a wonderful life.

Children were sent off with homilies about how to be successful in their new country from people who would never have dared leave their own home town. The illusion that migration was an exciting adventure was encouraged as this added to its appeal. The other approach was to emphasise a sense of spiritual duty: that sending children to Canada was part of God's purpose.

Until 1890, child migration was still smiled upon in Canada but then there was a slow build-up of hostility to migrant children, which rapidly increased towards the end of the century. In these years, when jobs were scarce and the scheme was criticised, supporters turned against it. Even then, the criticisms weren't directed towards the way the children were exploited but the social problems they were said to create.

In 1888, a member of Parliament for Welland, Ontario, called the migrants "the offal of the most depraved characters in the cities of the old country". It was as if he had lit a fire, and other critics rushed in to fan the flames. They all came up with the same conclusion: that "much crime, drunkenness and prostitution was seen as a result of the child migration scheme". Economically, child migrants flooded the labour market and drove down wages. Considering the children's pathetic lack of skills, this was a pretty unlikely argument but it was still often used.

Another criticism was that the migrant children were "morally unfit" to become companions of other children. Other Canadian children, that is. The migrant children were already only too well aware of the stigma of being a Home Child. They had to put up with much the same attitudes to "gutter children" and "paupers" in nineteenth-century Britain too. The children sent to Australia sixty years later – when the Children's Act of 1948 had been passed and the nation had welcomed child welfare – felt equally stigmatised. It is still not always recognised that all children forcibly and officially removed from their families and put in institutional care feel stigmatised in some way.

Some migrant children were naturally difficult to handle, but it's only extraordinary that so few of them were, given their circumstances and origins and the life they were expected to live in Canada. One girl of eleven who was sent to a family in Toronto for adoption but was sent back to the Home after a year, said:

> Maybe in those days I resented a lot of things. I could have been a little bit contrary, you get kind of bitter towards everybody when you are pushed around so much. And it was an awful hard blow when I had to leave my foster parents in London, they were very good to me.

Another criticism of the children was that their poor background would have a bad effect on the Canadian race. One man who supported this view was the physician Dr C. K. Clarke – who was to have the Clarke Institute in Toronto named after him. He publicly stated that:

> In Canada we are deliberately adding to our population hundreds of children bearing all the stigmata of physical and mental degeneracy . . . And this is being done openly and apparently with the consent of many who are really anxious to prove themselves philanthropists. I refer to the children who are brought to Canada in order to benefit themselves and the country.

Dr Clarke had been on a train with children who were being transported to a reception Home and to various farms. He said he was depressed at the sign of "degeneracy that was so obvious in those children", and said that the authorities were guilty of criminal neglect to allow them into the country. Others agreed with him. The London (Ontario) National Council of Women were convinced that child migrants were a real danger to Canadian stock and insisted that protection be guaranteed. Some claimed these children carried some dark defect in their bones which would lead to crime or insanity or both. The fear of syphilis happened to be strong then: even many medical men thought it could remain undetected in the body of a child and then be passed to other children in the family, or to close associates. Families were warned about taking in waifs in case they infected their own children.

The panic was stoked up by wild accusations from the local press. Whenever and wherever a child was involved in a crime, the criminal was immediately said to be a child migrant. Even children who committed suicide were seen as having criminal genes. No thought was given as to why they were led to such a desperate act or whether others were perhaps responsible – even though in one case there was clear evidence that the child had been repeatedly ill-treated.

A few local papers like the *Winnipeg Free Paper* protested that this moral panic was totally misplaced; that the children committing offences were rarely child migrants but local children. But the label stuck. Similar attitudes were to be found in Britain as this 1893 edition of *Highways and Hedges* (The National Children's Homes magazine) shows:

> For some of them are of poor human material; their constitution – physical and mental – is of inferior texture; they are naturally deficient in force of character and moral stamina; their antecedents were once vicious or at least unpromising; the sad entail of hereditary weakness or wickedness makes these unfortunate juveniles peculiarly the objects

of our compassionate and continuous care ... Canada is no place to shoot rubbish. It is a magnificent British colony waiting for development and capable of absorbing and enriching generations of children trained in habits of honest industry and good living.

The Canadians were also concerned about the way children were placed with families as they felt there was no real control over them. One suggestion was that they should all be placed in foster homes – not by the organisations bringing them from Britain but by newly formed Children's Aid Societies. This would effectively have meant handing over the children to the Canadian organisations and was hotly resisted by the British who feared, in turn, losing control. This was one reason why they began to turn their attention to other countries.

There was fierce pressure on the Canadian government to act over the issue of child migration and in 1897 it finally commissioned J. J. Kelso, a well-known figure in Canadian child welfare, to write "A Special Report on the Immigration of British Children." Kelso obviously did not want to offend the organisations who brought the children to Canada or the farmers who accepted them. His conclusion was bland: "Child immigration, if carried out with care and discretion, need not be injurious to the best interests of this country." He ducked the issue of how to protect abused children:

The charge is often made that this species of immigration is child slavery plain and simple, but there is no legitimate reason why this should be so. Farm work should be healthful and enjoyable employment for young people if the employers are reasonable and kindly disposed. Unfortunately there have in the past been cases brought to light forcibly illustrating the need for diligence in protecting children from cruel taskmasters, but there is hardly sufficient ground for the sweeping charge that this is the prevailing condition.

Nevertheless, Ontario and Manitoba passed laws regulating immigration. As most child migrants went to these two provinces, this legislation was important and annoyed the British organisations, who had had it all their own way until then. A typical reaction appeared in the magazine Our Waifs and Strays in December, 1898:

Section 12 of the Act passed last year by the Ontario legislature regulating the immigration into that Province of destitute and outcast children, it was made absolutely prohibitive to bring into the Province any child "who has been reared or who has resided amongst habitual criminals, or any child whose parents have been habitual criminals, lunatics or idiots, or weak-minded or defective constitutionally or confirmed paupers, or diseased", and any person bringing such a child in could be fined up to $100 or imprisoned for up to 3 months.

When it is remembered that emigration is often the sole hope for such children, and that in no other way can the contact with the former bad surroundings be broken, it was not to be wondered at that workers on this side considered that the Act would seriously interrupt, if not entirely paralyse, the efforts on behalf of this most unfortunate class of children.

Canadian inspection procedures were now also generally introduced and this, too, irritated the organisations in Britain, who regarded these as unnecessary – possibly because they had to bear most of the cost.

The effect of all this was dramatic. The number of children sent to Canada dropped from 3,015 a year in 1896 to 977 in 1900–1. But for the time being the numbers then started to rise again, slowly and then faster, over the twelve years or so until the First World War in 1914. The reports and fears were forgotten. The 1906 report by the Departmental Committee on Agricultural Settlement in British Colonies, for instance, comfortably dismissed Andrew Doyle's criticisms as no longer valid!

> In former years, indeed, objections were made – not without reason – to the whole system of juvenile emigration on the grounds of insufficiency of inspection: but these wise and stringent regulations made since then by the authorities both here and in Canada, have in our opinion removed all cause for complaint.

Nevertheless, child migration was becoming the subject of overall strong criticism. In the 1920s, the British magazine *John Bull* offered examples of the cruelty with which some of the child migrants had been treated in Canada, under headlines such as "Appalling Child Slavery". Eventually, a committee was appointed in England to "obtain first-hand information with regard to the system of child migration and settlement in Canada". It was headed by Margaret Bondfield and reported in December 1924.

The result was another bland affair favouring child migration, for the Committee came out with all the tired old clichés; it was satisfied, it said, that great care was exercised by those who placed the children on the farms, though the method of selection was not always up to standard. On the whole, the Committee said soothingly, the children were well placed and treated with kindness and consideration. It was satisfied, too, that at all times the children were carefully and appropriately inspected and had a good future.

We have no doubt that the prospects in Canada for the average boy or girl are better than they would be in the U.K. . . . As regards the girls, the majority of them marry and settle down satisfactorily within the country as farmers' wives or in the towns . . .

That same year, the *Evening Telegram* of St John's, Newfoundland carried a report about the "Harsh and Cowardly Treatment of Immigrant Boy". Though censured for neglecting and ill-treating a British child migrant, the farmer concerned was acquitted of manslaughter on the grounds that "there was no legal responsibility to provide medical attendance and care".

Only briefly did the Committee waver and that was over the problem of the younger children, concluding:

It seems to us, recognising that the children are sent to Canada for working purposes, the general principle to be adopted is that the children should not leave the country until they have arrived at working age.

Earlier arguments that said the younger the children were sent, the better, were ignored or forgotten. The recommendation was accepted by Britain and Canada, with Canada making an Order in Council banning child migrants under fourteen. In the autumn of 1925 it was claimed that the very last party of young children was leaving Britain for Canada.

6

Bricks for Empire Building

Come cheer up, my lads, the
    way groweth clear
To migrate some more in this
    glorious year;
To the Empire we call you, free men,
    not slaves,
You will enjoy the life o'er
    the waves.

The glorious year was 1912, the date was 24 April, and "Lads for the Empire" (above) was lustily sung at a meeting advertised as a "Great Mass Meeting on Junior Imperial Migration". "Land of Hope and Glory" was on the agenda, so was "God Save the King", and a streamer of bunting proclaimed, "One King, One Flag, One Empire". A *Daily Sketch* photo of boys cheering the King was captioned: "300 British working lads sail for Australia. Before sailing they sent a telegram to the King pledging their loyalty."

The youngsters signing up were filled with the same kind of fervour and patriotism as those who, in just a couple of years, would be signing up as volunteers for the trenches. There should have been a Kitchener poster saying, "Your country needs *you* to emigrate."

In the nineteenth century, child migrants were shipped off for ostensibly philanthropic reasons, to protect them from the evils of their environment in Britain. But in the twentieth century, philanthropy took second place to unadulterated imperialism. Child migrants were thought of as "Bricks for Empire Building". The main reason for this was the Boer War in South Africa which ended in 1902. Only by repopulating the Empire with British stock could the damaging effects of this war be repaired. A strong British presence would also help quell any future insurgency in the ranks. One of the most active promoters of this belief and the organiser of the Great Mass Meeting, was Thomas Sedgwick, a social worker, who took his first party of fifty lads to New Zealand to do farm work on 9 December 1910.

He wrote an unusually truthful letter to them all before they left, explaining that as it was an experiment they had better understand the conditions facing them:

> The LIFE will be found hard, rough, monotonous and dull. There are no lighted streets, shops, theatres etc in the county districts, and the nearest neighbour is sometimes ten miles off. Work begins at 4 am and much farm-work has to be done on Sundays.
> ... There is no work in towns and the lads will have to do the HOUSEWORK as well as FARM WORK for the employers . . .
> Beyond 1/- a week pocket money, they will probably only earn enough during the first year to repay their fare. The balance of wages (less the fares) will be banked by the employers and paid after the end of the apprenticeship.

When they finally went aboard, Sedgwick proudly sent a message to the King:

> The first party of town lads for colonial farms beg to convey to Your Majesty the expression of our most dutiful and humble devotion to your Throne and person on our departure for the Dominion of New Zealand.

Sedgwick delighted himself by placing his fifty lads in jobs and wrote enthusiastically that "at least 10,000 lads could be absorbed every year on the land in New Zealand, Australia and Canada, where wages and conditions of life are far better than here . . . and equal number of girls could also be placed out in good homes as domestic servants each year . . ." It was a letter that could have been written by Maria Rye, Annie Macpherson, Barnardo, Fairbridge – any or all of them. He continued to take boys to New Zealand, convinced he was doing sterling work for the Empire despite the remarks of any foolish critics. The New Zealand magazine, *Truth,* was one of these. In an article called "Sedgwick's striplings", it said:

> When the proposal was first mooted to introduce boy slavery from England to this youthful Dominion . . . a seasonable word was said by this journal for the unhappy youngsters torn from charitable institutions in the old world, shipped to a new country, and imposed upon by farmer persons who are ever on the look-out for cheap labour. These wretched youths have no friends, they are apprenticed . . . for a number of years at a microscopic screw without having any say in the matter and if they attempt to break from their horrible surroundings,

they will be hauled before a magistrate and either sent back to their taskmasters or suffer gaol.

But Sedgwick could comfort himself with polite notes from Buckingham Palace, plaudits from the *Sunday Express* and a letter from Francis, Cardinal Bourne, which referred to his self-sacrificing efforts in apprenticing youths from the old country to farmers in New Zealand. The letter ended, "I consider the work you are doing to be of the highest possible value."

Sedgwick started his activities at approximately the same time as the Child Emigration Society was set up by Kingsley Fairbridge. He started the society after a vision that came to him one summer's day in Rhodesia which he describes in his autobiography:

When you close your eyes on a hot day you may see things that have remained half hidden at the back of your brain. That day I saw a street in the East End of London. It was a street crowded with children – dirty children, yet lovable, exhausted with the heat. No decent air, not enough food. The waste of it all! Children's lives wasting while the Empire cried out for more. There were work-houses full – and no farmers. "Farmers – children, farmers – children" . . . the words ran in my head.

The vision began to turn into something more specific:

Train the children to be farmers! Not in England. Teach them their farming in the land where they will farm . . . Shift the orphanages of Britain, north, south, east and west to the shores of Greater Britain (the Empire) where farmers and farmers' wives are wanted, and where no man with strong arms and a willing heart would ever want for his daily bread . . .

I saw great Colleges of Agriculture (not workhouses) springing up in every man-hungry corner of the Empire. I saw little children shedding the bondage of bitter circumstances and stretching their legs amid the thousand interests of the farm. I saw waste turned to providence, the waste of unneeded humanity converted to the husbandry of unpeopled acres. This is a great thing, I thought: I must think it over. I must be cautious. It is all so plain – so simple. I may be mistaken on some points. But if I am right I will put this thing before the people of England – so help me God.

Like so many before him, Fairbridge linked the unwanted children in Britain to the emptiness of the Empire. He wanted to believe there was a small, enticing gap that could readily be filled, and resolved any doubts about the validity of this idea this way:

Always I comforted myself, thinking of the children who would be happier, of the bare acres that would bloom . . . I would look into the deep valleys where the grass was six feet high and wish I could see a farm. I imagined smoke coming out of the chimney and the grass all cropped by cattle. I spoke it out aloud. "Someday I will bring farmers here".

Fairbridge was fired into translating his dream into reality. An intense British patriot, he had an iron will and in 1909, supported by friends and his future wife Ruby, he gave an impassioned speech to the Colonial Club at Oxford, describing his dream. Such was his certainty about the merits of child migration that every man there promptly enrolled as a member of the "Society for the Furtherance of Child Emigration to the Colonies." He argued that Great Britain and Greater Britain were interdependent, one entity. The colonies had the land and Britain the men – though not always the type needed in the colonies. Orphaned and poor children, said Fairbridge, should therefore be trained in schools of agriculture in the colonies.

In October 1909, the Premier of Western Australia was in London for King George V's coronation and, impressed by Fairbridge, made him an attractive offer of land and other facilities. "So it was," said Fairbridge, that "the newest of new farm colonies became the home of the first farm school." The first party of thirteen children, aged between seven and thirteen, arrived in January 1913 to find a rather run-down farm of 160 acres, four miles out of Pinjarra, Western Australia. Four months later a second party of twenty-two boys arrived (the school was later to move to a nearby, much larger site). It was the beginning of Fairbridge's own small empire, although only after his death was another farm school opened in Molong, New South Wales. Farm schools were also opened in two other countries: in Vancouver Island, Canada, in 1935; and in Rhodesia in 1946 (see Chapter 8).

It was interesting that a farm school should open in Canada, despite that country's Order in Council banning child migrants under fourteen. But the Fairbridge children, aged seven and upwards, were, it seemed, not child migrants. They were the sound British stock and were "farm trainees" and as such were welcomed by Canada. There was one protest; but it was not for the sake of the children. The Canadian Daughters' League telegraphed the capital, Ottawa, to say:

In view of present destitute Saskatchewan settlers asking relief and tremendous numbers of young men in relief camps we strongly protest allowing into Canada British waifs and strays for training in

Fairbridge farm schools located in Vancouver Island. What guarantee has Canada that these immigrants will never become public charges?

Fairbridge's dream of great colleges of agriculture was summed up more succinctly by his wife, who described the aims of these farm schools in her biography of her husband:

> The whole *raison d'etre* of a farm school was to teach boys to be farmers or skilled farm hands and the girls to be helpful partners and assistants.

The idea of farm schools was by no means new; Barnardo had built one in Russell, Manitoba, many years earlier. One of their major disadvantages was that they were all set in the open countryside, isolated from people. Children, faced with their new surroundings usually in the middle of nowhere, were often totally bewildered.

George Wilkins, aged eleven, for instance, was one of the early arrivals at the Fairbridge Farm School in Molong, New South Wales, Australia, and he thought it was appalling – in the middle of nowhere. As the bus drove him up the long, dusty road to the farm school, he planned an escape route, memorising every bend in the road. But escape was a dream. There was nowhere to go and no one to go to. Those who did try to run away were soon caught:

> They would be taken into the assembly room and everyone in the school would be called in by the head. The runaways would then be publicly thrashed, usually six thrashes with the canes. They'd have the welts on their behinds for days like badges of their misbehaviour. It certainly put me off running away.

For children to be happy and cared for in any institution, it is crucial that the quality of care is good. At the farm schools, the staff had sometimes undergone a short training period but they weren't professional child-carers. Fairbridge instituted the "cottage" scheme in which children lived in various cottages, with British names like Shakespeare and Raleigh. About fifteen to twenty children were allocated to a cottage and each cottage was single sex. Brothers and sisters were separated to different parts of the farm, seeing each other only once a month, even though stress was laid on the importance of family togetherness: if a child had any brothers or sisters, they were all encouraged to come out. Of course there was the occasional slip-up. Molly Whyte Harris, who runs the Old Fairbridgean Association in Vancouver, recalled that:

> One of the boys sent to Canada found out after thirty-five years that his youngest brother, who had the measles and had not accompanied

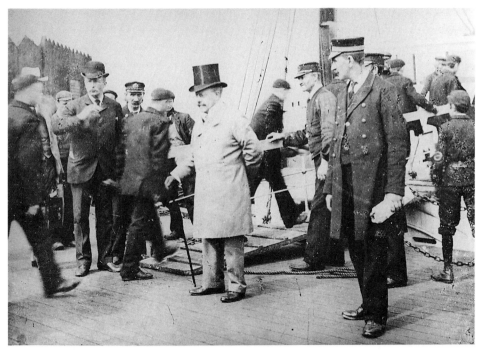

Dr Barnardo sees his boys off to Canada.
(*Barnardo Photographic Archive*)

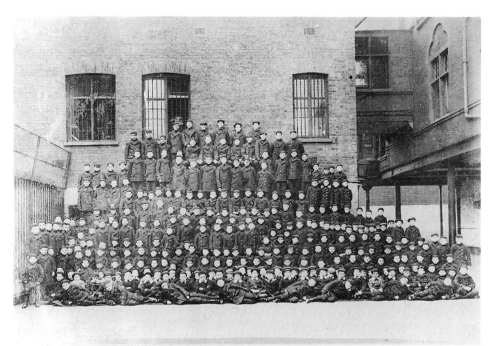

An early group of emigrants from Dr Barnardo's Home in Stepney, east London.
(*Barnardo Photographic Archive*)

A party of Barnardo's girls arriving in Quebec, 1912.   (*Barnardo Photographic Archive*)

Barnardo boys working on a farm in Canada in about 1912.   (*Barnardo Photographic Archive*)

him, was sent to the Australian [Fairbridge] school at Molong by mistake. A typing error, perhaps.

The children in cottages were looked after by cottage "mothers". Some were kind women, who would genuinely try to help the children come to terms with the upheaval they had gone through in coming thousands of miles away from home. But some cottage mothers turned out to be totally unsuitable for the job of looking after children. One boy who went to the Fairbridge Farm School at Molong, recalls that:

> Some of the cottage mothers were very brutal. There was no selection process in their choice and some of them were often under the influence of alcohol, striking out at whatever child was closest with whatever object was nearest. There was an inquiry, for example, into the house mother who used to horsewhip the children in her house. Some of the boys got really badly hurt and maimed. There was an investigation, but she was still there at the end of it.

Another compared his cottage mother in Fairbridge Farm School, Vancouver Island in Canada, to Attila the Hun:

> She was just mean, a mean woman. She was Scottish and hefty and cuffed us around and made us work for everything. Yes, I was unhappy there but with me it was a way of life. I did not know any different. You would not realise you were unhappy, you just thought, I am here with a bunch of kids, this is it. If you had a mother and father and were taken away from them, you were naturally unhappy.

Ironically, having a cottage mother who favoured you didn't always work out that well either, as an eight year old found out:

> I recollect once getting beat up by the kids and I got a whipping by the headmaster as well as being beaten up by the rest. My brother spent a lot of time fighting on my behalf. Because I was so young [eight years] the cottage mother sort of favoured me, which did not sit well with the other kids. And school was very strict. I told a stupid lie and because of it I wasn't able to go swimming for a week. I had bruises right down from my knee from the beating. A high rate did run away, but came back because they had nowhere else to go.

Some boys, on the other hand, praised their cottage mothers extravagantly. One boy looked on her as his mother, taking his fiancée to her for approval. This particular cottage mother left the boy all her possessions. But as one Fairbridge boy said:

> What worries me about places like that [farm schools, homes, orphanages] is that I feel you need people there who really understand

kids and who will give them the affection that they may have missed. You need extraordinarily good people in those places, not just anyone you can pick up on the street. That means money, you know. And I think they're [carers] fairly low priority stuff: "OK, we'll look after these kids but we're not going to spend a fortune on it." Well, in many respects I think we need to spend money on kids who may ultimately become anti-social because they've never known affection.

Molly Whyte Harris remembers the staff with fondness, "They were just so close to us and so kind to us and they still are." While she has been running the Old Fairbridgeans in British Columbia, she has held occasional reunions and says, "We children, we have a bond, we are closer to one another even though not related because we did everything together at school." This was strikingly evident at one reunion of Old Fairbridgeans at Pinjarra. Many there were in tears as they met each other again and looked at old photos. They had no photos of their own family; plucked from home, the farm school was the only family they ever knew. The old boys occasionally come down at weekends to repair the buildings.

Some don't want to look back on their Fairbridge childhood. One who went to Fairbridge Farm School in Vancouver Island said:

I think there are only good new days, I don't believe in good old days. What's the point in thinking of Fairbridge if it wasn't any fun? When they said we are having a reunion, well, I have blanked it out of my mind. I have been back there at various times, when the cottages were there, but empty. Next time, all the cottages were falling apart. I often said I was going to buy a lot out there, it's a beautiful spot. I don't feel that I have a past, I have no photos, recollections.

Others, with generous memories, react defensively to implied criticism, waving the Fairbridge flag years after. One man, now a professor in South Korea, says:

The majority of us are not at all bitter about our experiences, but rather profoundly grateful to Kingsley Fairbridge for his wonderful scheme. Many of us have found our UK roots – many still wish to find them, though satisfied with our life otherwise.

Another, who went to Molong agreed that:

It would be very wrong to paint Fairbridge as being some kind of black hole back in the fifties and sixties. The whole ethos that pervaded child care in those days was very different from today. I think all child care then could have been a lot better run. It needed more money; it needed better people to run it; it needed a set of humanising values.

The Fairbridge Farm School at Duncan, Vancouver Island, Canada, is an example of how these farm schools were run. It had a day school on the site, a chapel and hospital, four small single cottages and four single houses. There were about 125 children at any one time and about forty staff. It was a seventy-acre self-sufficient farm, like those in Australia, and the farm work was almost entirely done by the children. In 1944, for example, there were about seventy dairy cows, 600 hens, 800 chicks and fifty-four pigs. The boys learnt how to do farm work; the girls, domestic work. Despite this, not a single boy shipped out there to farm has become a farmer.

One boy who went out there in 1937 when he was seven, remembers doing "everything" on the farm. "You cleaned the horse stalls, chopped wood, weeded the garden, milked the cows." The earlier child migrants to Canada did the same kind of work but in isolation. Another, who came out in 1946 when he was eight, recalls:

Everyone had chores, milking cows, feeding chickens. Virtually anything you would do on a farm. The animals were top-grade stuff: pure-bred Clydesdales, blue ribbon horses, chickens. I do remember, in the Fall, we used to go out and act as bird dogs and scare birds out of the bush and the local people out hunting would give us hot dogs. We used to play ice hockey on ponds that had frozen. We would fish using a pole with a pin on it.

There were no holidays. At Christmas we were allowed to pick something out of the Sears catalogue for a dollar. Other than that, it was a pretty routine life. On 24 May, the Queen's birthday, we used to go down to Victoria and we had a Fairbridge band and it would play. Every year there was a five mile cross-country race and they used to give us a lump of brown sugar to give us energy and I just remember getting lost and nearly trampled on.

In the summer they used to bring in a bulldozer to bulldoze gravel and form a swimming pool in the river and we used to go there and swim. In winter, there was not a lot of snow here. But I could hardly wait until I was twelve when I could get a pair of long pants. It was cold otherwise.

Not quite as much money, it would seem, was spent on the children as on the well-bred animals. A woman who was a nurse there in 1940, remembers:

Fairbridge was given an ancient dental chair with no electric power. Dr Kenneth Murchie [the dentist] came from Duncan twice a month, I think, to attend to the children. The drill was operated by a foot treadle. It was so difficult for the poor dentist to have both hands busy and one foot operating the treadle that I used to treadle for him, when I wasn't making fillings under his direction.

One of the first arrivals in 1935 – five years before the dental chair appeared – was a nine-year-old girl who remembers the group having the school to themselves for nearly two years "because it took that long to clear the land and for the accommodation to be built". Describing her daily life there, she says:

We had a routine. We were got up at six and would have to take turns in setting up to start the furnace. It needed wood and we would chop it. Each girl would make her own bed and sweep the dormitory, so it would be neat and clean: this was our training. And then we would go to the main dining hall and we all ate in the one great big dining room, with long, long tables. We had our time for school and time for work: we all had our duties. Then everyone would go to their individual cottages to make their own supper: boys and girls were also trained to do their own mending and darning. After supper we would go to the playing fields and we girls would be playing grass hockey. We were always the champs as we had nothing else to do. There were no distractions, like in a private home. We did not really feel Canadian: everything was English to us.

But the Fairbridge March carried a different message:

> Cheerio!
> Here we are
> Working hard
> On the land
> On our Fairbridge Farm.
>
> Cheerio!
> Here we are
> Learning hard
> The golden rule
> At the Fairbridge School.
>
> Cheerio!
> Here we are
> Playing hard
> In the fields
> Where the skylarks sing
> As we stroll along the country lane
> And singing on our way
> For we love our Island home
> In Canada
> Our Empire home
> For we love our Island home
> Our Empire home in Canada.
> God bless our home in Canada
> And bless our Fairbridge School

> God bless our Alma Mater
> Where we learn the golden rule
> God bless our home in Canada
> And may we always sing
> The Maple Leaf, O Canada
> God save our Gracious King

This girl left the farm school at fourteen, as they all did, and was sent to work for a prominent family.

> They were very snobbish, reacted as if I was from the gutter and I couldn't believe that someone could act that way. I was working there from six in the morning until eleven at night because they entertained all the time. The matron would come to see how we were doing and I would be sobbing to her, telling her how miserable I was. And she would say, "Oh, well, you can stick it out."

One Fairbridge boy was conscious of the way class was an integral part of the whole scheme:

> There's a lot of empire-type stuff associated with Fairbridge. There were people in London who were trying to do the right thing. It was a kind of *noblesse oblige*, wasn't it. "Let's look after the unfortunate kids from the working classes." It's all very well for, say, someone from middle or upper middle class background to say these kids need this or that. And to do that we need to remove them from their circumstances . . . But removing kids from their roots I think is a very serious step to take indeed. If we look back historically, it was kind of misguided. It might salve one's conscience to have these Homes where you can put these kids away and give them a Christmas present and dress them up and so forth, but I don't know whether that's the ultimate answer.

Fairbridge himself had no such doubts. At the time he went up to Oxford to make his rousing speech about sending children to the far-flung outposts of the Empire like burnt offerings, he could have drawn on some 300 years of experience in child migration. But he never made any serious investigations into its history: he was apparently oblivious to previous criticisms. Perhaps it was central to his makeup to ignore these crucial past experiences and the impact of earlier projects. Visionaries rarely listen to others.

Fairbridge stressed that the farm schools were no charitable undertaking but an "imperial investment". There would therefore be no shame in being a pauper, every child would be proud to be representing England. This was not so. Fairbridge children, like Barnardo's and others before them, carried with them the stigma of being unwanted. Fairbridge prided himself on being concerned with education, saying:

> In a vast community like Great Britain thousands of children are born every day, who by the death of one – or perhaps both of their parents, are left homeless and destitute. We leave these little orphans in the workhouse, we do not give them a chance. We do not give education a chance, wide far-seeing education, by the educated, based on handicrafts and land culture.

On paper this sounds splendid. Who would want to leave little orphans in a workhouse when they could be learning land culture in an agricultural college? But the education these children received at the farm schools was aimed to raise them no higher than farmers, farm labourers, domestic servants. Only a few of the brighter middle or upper class children got preferential treatment and a higher level of education.

George Wilkins was only the third boy from Molong to be sent to the local high school in the nearby town of Orange. But though lucky to get much more education than the other child migrants at Molong, he found he was an outsider at the high school. He didn't fit in. He had no school uniform, no school books and no money for school outings.

> I remember being humiliated in assembly soon after I started. The headmaster shouted out in front of the whole school, "Why is that boy not wearing uniform?" I always felt uncomfortable because I didn't have any uniform. I never fitted in and I couldn't take part in school activities because I had no money for that. Then there was no time for homework 'cause when I got back in the evening I had to do my tasks around the farm. And I felt an outsider there too because the other boys and girls resented the fact that I didn't do as much work on the farm as they did. I remember being made to work on Christmas day to compensate for the occasional task I had missed because of going to high school.
>
> When I first went to the high school, I did fairly well, but gradually I went backwards. By my fourth year I was bottom by far. I got two per cent in one exam and the second from bottom got forty per cent. I had no choice but to leave. I felt demoralised by the whole experience.

George Wilkins went on to become a millionaire but says fiercely that he did it in spite of Fairbridge, rather than because of it.

Many agencies, including Fairbridge, arranged that children should have a proportion of their wages sent to the agency and kept until they were twenty-one, when they could reclaim this lump sum. Inevitably, however, particularly with the early Canadian migrants, the children lost touch and failed to do so. As one woman, who went to Fairbridge Farm School in Vancouver Island, said, "Half your wages would go back to the school and it was put into a bank account for you until you were twenty-one. I got mine, but an awful lot of the children say they did not and I suppose it was because they did not write for it. The auditors that were handling our books, they say it is now all just dusty files. That money is lost, but where is the interest? I know there is a lot of bitterness from some of the kids."

This same farm school was financially aided by people in Britain and Canadian businessmen. When the property and land were sold, the money went back to the society in England with an "understanding" the money would go towards setting up a scholarship for the Fairbridge children's children, if they needed help. But nothing happened. As one Old Fairbridgean said, "If the sale of the land is actually rightfully ours, what is the hesitation about getting it back to us?"

The First World War brought child migration to a temporary halt and interrupted Fairbridge's plans to develop more farm schools. He fell out with the Australian government, who were becoming less and less keen on the idea and, with the contributions of his Oxford friends drying up, it looked at one stage as if the project would close. An annual report of the Fairbridge Society said:

> The land too had proved disappointing. Local knowledge is needed to enable one to select wisely and lacking that knowledge he had established himself on unsuitable country.

But due to Fairbridge's eloquence, the demand for migrants to Australia after the First World War and the help of grants, the project survived and for a time even prospered. Kingsley Fairbridge died on 19 July 1924. A note at the end of his autobiography says:

> Kingsley's health began to fail. He lived however to see part of his dream come true. He saw 200 children from many a dark and dreary back street, brimful of happiness, enjoying the ever varied teeming interests of a farm. He saw his old boys returning, men now, and some of them owning their own land: they one and all said "We thank you".

One and all? Not perhaps Violet Davis, who lost the sight of one eye due to a careless accident with ether in the school "hospital". Or her husband Francis who on leaving Pinjarra, was sent by Fairbridge to Bruce Rock, some 200 miles east of Perth, to be a farm hand, where the farmer, an MP and well-respected figure, made him live in a hut by the stables and worked him dawn to dusk with no reprieve. For this Francis was paid virtually nothing. Or Len Phenna, denied access to critical information that would have enabled him to trace his family, whose mind is now almost obsessed by the need to find information about his father.

A few years after Fairbridge's death, the Duke and Duchess of York paid a visit to Pinjarra and expressed their appreciation and admiration, "especially remarking on the superior tone". The Duke of York said:

> I, for one, cannot say too much in favour of the Fairbridge Farm School as I have seen it in operation. I only wish that there were more Farm Schools all over Australia and other parts of the Empire – but they must be run on the Fairbridge principle. Environment must play a tremendous part in our lives and these children, transplanted from the playground of the street to the beauty and healthiness of Australia with its enormous possibilities, will live to bless the name of Kingsley Fairbridge.

The Prince of Wales was also to add his praise:

> I have had the opportunity of going to Western Australia myself . . . the society is working most certainly on the right lines, to develop migration within the Empire and to relieve the sadly overcrowded areas and congestion of population in our country. I hope . . . that in years to come the society will be able to extend its efforts in all our Dominions.

In 1922, the Premier of South Australia proposed taking 6,000 child migrants from Britain. The British government was delighted. It was suggested in Parliament that the Boards of Guardians used their funds to send more children to Australia.

> If this were done it would relieve the State of a certain amount of money for the public purse, and also provide Canada and Australia with a very large number of juvenile immigrants.

There were two reasons why the Premier wanted 6,000 child migrants. After the heavy Australian casualties of the First World War, male emigrants were needed to replace them. Also, there was a growing fear in Australia that the country was going to be overrun by Asians from the north, particularly from China. The general feeling was that if the White Australia Policy was going to be preserved, there had better be a fast influx of migrants from Britain to boost the Anglo-Saxon stock.

So migration schemes to Australia took off after 1918. Fairbridge took advantage of the outstretched Australian hand and so did Barnardo's, who sent out more children than any other organisation. All got assistance towards the cost of a child's passage and grants from both the United Kingdom government, and the relevant Commonwealth one, towards capital costs.

The first of Barnardo's many groups left in 1921. The patriotic drum was beaten in Australia as well as Britain and when this group arrived in Adelaide in 1921, they were told by the State Governor, "You must remember the 61,000 who gave their lives for Australia in the last war. You will help replace them, and I am perfectly sure you realise what your duty to Australia is."

The "Millions Clubs" were set up with the slogan "A Million Migrants for Australia", and the Big Brother movement was formed in 1925 in New South Wales (and returned in Tasmania in 1948 when there was another push for British migrants). The idea was simple. An established Australian acted as "Big Brother" to a British boy aged between sixteen and seventeen, who got an assisted passage. Encouragement was given to "any intelligent youth who wants ultimately to farm on his own account". Big Brother committees in Australia then found the migrant a good home and arranged for him to be visited at work. His own personal Big Brother kept in touch, offering a short-term home or holiday accommodation, until he was settled. The Director of Child Welfare in Sydney was the legal custodian of each boy until he reached twenty-one. The scheme didn't always work out, as Big Brothers sometimes gave inadequate help. But unlike most child migrants, the boys were older and at least had some choice in the decision to emigrate.

It was in the inter-war years that the Roman Catholic teaching Order of Christian Brothers first opened orphanages in Western Australia to receive boys from Roman Catholic Homes in the United Kingdom. Their appeal for funds said:

> It is expected that before the end of the present year, 1938, over one hundred English Catholic children will have been immigrated to Western Australia, and it is confidently hoped that each succeeding year will add considerably to the number, and by this means it is hoped that the Child Emigration Scheme will do much to build up a Greater England in the island continent of the Southern Hemisphere by peopling it with religious-minded, efficient and devoted citizens.

One of the orphanages was the isolated St Joseph's Farm School, at Bindoon, set in 17,000 acres of land sixty miles north of Perth; another was St Mary's Agricultural School, Tardun, which was over 300 miles from Perth. The pamphlets on these orphanages made them sound a riot of fun and sun.

The English children will be placed in the country of their adoption during their tender and most impressionable years, in very congenial and happy surroundings, and in a land of sunshine and plenty. They will live with, and be educated side by side with Australian-born children and be trained by religious teachers; they will have free access to the thousands of acres of land belonging to the Institutions and which the boys love to call *our own paddocks,* as each proudly feels that he is a partner in the great scheme . . .

Omitted from these pamphlets were the sexual abuse and cruelty which some young children sent out to these orphanages experienced (see Chapters 1 and 9). Isolated as they were, no word of what was happening got out. And still the children came. Thousands more were sent out by the Catholic organisations than by any other agency.

South Africa, watching the flow of child migrants change direction from Canada to Australia, and to a lesser extent Rhodesia, wanted to divert them through its own doors. Barnardo had briefly considered the country after the Boer War but the post-war economy was unstable and the relationship between the British settlers and the Boers remained too bitter for the scheme to be a success.

Nevertheless, for all these countries, it was open house on British children. The British government, always eager to save costs at home at the expense of colonial governments abroad, cheered on the children. The voluntary societies collected the subsidies and, under no constraints whatsoever, made their decisions about the type of regime under which the children should be brought up.

Few curbs were placed on them and there was not a hint of a code of good practice. There were no objective arrangements to inspect the children's progress; to check on their happiness; to give them access to personal and family records; to arrange for them to be sent home if they could not settle and had a parent or parents in Britain; to educate them well enough to get a professional job; to provide after-care.

The children boarding the emigration ships were often cheered off by classmates at the boat. Listening to an account of what happened to one child in Australia many years later, a horrified teacher said, "Oh, my God, if only we'd known. There we all were, waving and thinking that they were all going off to this better world."

That, too, is what the children thought.

7

The Wartime Rush

Winston Churchill was against sending children overseas at the start of the war. He thought it could lead to "a movement of such dimensions that a crop of alarmist and depressive rumours would follow at its tail, detrimental to the interest of national defence".

Nevertheless, in 1939, as concern over the war grew, some 100,000 parents applied to have their children taken from Britain to safety abroad. Children were already being evacuated into the countryside at home but at this stage only the better-off parents could afford to send their children overseas. They paid their children's passage themselves and also made arrangements about where their children should stay. Canadian families were among the first to offer their homes and the newspapers were full of happy-looking children across the Atlantic. Sometimes firms in Britain arranged for the children of their employees to go to their overseas branches. One boy, who was only two when the war started, and was later to go to a Fairbridge school in Rhodesia, said:

> My two brothers went to the States at the beginning of the war, I think it was through Hoover where my father worked, and I did not see them for twenty-five years. I was still in England, too young to be evacuated.

Many Britons thought it totally unfair that only wealthier children could be spirited to safety overseas, while children from poor families had to stay in Britain and endure the deprivation and dangers of war in Europe. The British government therefore set up a scheme jointly with the Dominions and the United States to select a limited number of children from all classes but mainly from state-aided schools, to go overseas for the duration of the war. To run it, the Children's Overseas Reception Board (CORB or CORB Limeys as it was sometimes called) was established. CORB was to select the children, see that they were properly equipped, organise their passage overseas, find the most suitable home for each child and arrange for the care, supervision and education of the children in their new homes until the conflict was over. Despite the 100,000 or so parents who applied, only about 15,000 to 20,000 children actually went.

The children were aged between five and fifteen and travelled on their own – no parents or guardians being allowed to go with them. They had trustworthy escorts: CORB advertised for volunteers and checked them carefully.

It was a new type of approach. But this overseas evacuation was different from child migration in three important ways: first, child evacuees left home only because of a serious risk to their safety; secondly, they went to families; thirdly, their parents agreed to them going because they expected to be reunited at the end of the war. This account by a woman who took over a group of sixteen children to Fairbridge Farm School in Vancouver Island in 1941, sums up the difference:

> To them, it was a kind of adventure, because they really did not have anything they cared about that they were leaving. They were not particularly happy where they were and a lot had no memories of anything. But they were not aware of the significance of it all: what does an eight year old really understand about what is happening?
>
> Some of them were very unhappy. One girl knew that her mother had given her up, sent her to this Emigration Home, and she was old enough to understand something of that. All the children were very seasick. The people on the ship were fantastically kind and that contributed to some of their seasickness, as they were not used to the kind of food they were being given.
>
> Some had brothers and sisters there [the farm school], so there would be some kind of reunion. But for some, they were just plucked out and sent to Duncan, the girls as domestics and the boys as farmworkers.
>
> We landed first in Quebec and then sailed on to Montreal and took the train across the continent and the kids were still train sick. Five days and five nights by train; many had never been on one before.

The evacuation of children abroad went on until October 1940 and the only reason it stopped then was because it was no longer safe to send children overseas. Early on in the war, the *Vollendam* was torpedoed and sunk. Although, through CORB, it was totally filled with children going to Canada, miraculously they were all saved after spending only a few hours in lifeboats. It created a spurious sense of safety which was shattered when, in September 1940, the *City of Benares* was sunk and hundreds of children were drowned. In Elspeth Huxley's book, *Atlantic Ordeal: the story of Mary Cornish*, Mary Cornish (who was acting as an escort to fifteen girls) describes the initial happiness of the ninety child evacuees on board, secure in the knowledge that they were going on an extended trip, but would return:

> Canada grew real in their imaginations, a glittering vision of the best that they had known in their own country. They talked continually of what they would do on their birthdays in a Canada of bigger cakes, brighter candles and creamier ices. One boy, going out to relatives, knew of a pony there; for him a ride was to be the birthday's greatest treat.

When the ship was torpedoed, all ninety children bar seven were drowned. The seven who survived spent over a week in a lifeboat before being picked up. The horror in Britain at this loss of young life effectively put paid to evacuating any more children as the Government immediately suspended its scheme. Some children, however, continued to go through private arrangement. The Fairbridge Society also considered it safe for child migrants to keep crossing the Atlantic. The woman who took over the group to Fairbridge Farm School in Vancouver Island recalled:

> It was one of the first crossings after the *Benares* was sunk. Each adult had only four children to look after, in order to teach them all how to deal with the lifeboats and so on. It was said that some of the children in the *Benares* were sitting on top of provisions in a life boat and did not even know they were there.

There was a clear difference between the CORB scheme, with its in-built, individual protection for the children on arrival, and the cavalier way so many thousands of child migrants had been shipped off to Canada. The crucial distinction, however, was the legal one. Under CORB, there were debates over the question of guardianship. For instance, what authority did the foster parents have over the children placed in their charge? What were the legal liabilities? Supposing the child required emergency medical treatment or died while getting it? Could the birth parents sue the foster parents and doctor as a result? What if the child was extremely hard to control and needed strict discipline? Could the foster parents administer it? And what if the child was subjected to abuse?

In all the years of child migration, no one had ever given a thought to the children's legal rights – to human rights. The rights, for example, of the girl at Fairbridge Farm School in Pinjarra who lost an eye, the boy at Bindoon Boys' Town in Western Australia who was deliberately knocked off scaffolding by one of the Christian Brothers or the boy on a farm in Ontario whose toes swelled up so badly the doctor wanted to amputate them, but who was finally treated with horse liniment. (Even today they are still melded together.)

None of these children got or will ever get, any legal compensation or acknowledgement. Unlike the wartime evacuees, they had no guardians to watch over their welfare. The child migrant, in any case, had no understanding of the law and was in no position to approach anyone if he had.

In New Zealand, legal guardianship of the wartime evacuees was the responsibility of the Department of Education. South Africa and Australia passed their own Guardianship Law. Canada and the United States were covered by the Temporary Migration of Children Act, 1940, which gave the British Secretary of State the legal right to appoint Lord Halifax as guardian for all British children in the United States and Malcolm MacDonald as guardian for them in Canada. Both men were the sole guardians of the children's welfare and could carry out their duties in accordance with British law.

When the war ended, most of the evacuee children returned, a few remaining with their foster parents abroad. When they did, they had to reintegrate themselves with family, friends and neighbourhood and, for some children, this was difficult. Their life had been so different abroad that parents, who had had to put up with the austerity of Britain, almost resented this. The children, too, had divided loyalties and found it hard to resettle.

Child migrants, of course, had no such problems; they were never to return. One of the main results of evacuation, in the meantime at any rate, was to make people look at the effect on children of being separated from their parents, even if just temporarily, and on the parents themselves. But no sooner was the war over than child migrants were once again sent off to Canada, Australia, New Zealand and, for the first time in large numbers, to Rhodesia. The same old arguments for sending the children were brought out, the same mistakes were still made.

8

Out to Africa

On 18 November 1946, a news item in the *Daily Graphic* read:

> His eyes bright with excitement, 13 year old Brian of Bell Lane, Enfield, Middlesex, said goodbye to his mother, father and three brothers at Rhodesia House, London, yesterday and started off on the first stage of a journey to Induna, Southern Rhodesia.
>
> Brian was thrilled because he is one of 18 British boys who are emigrating to Rhodesia to be educated at the Fairbridge Memorial College. All expenses will be borne.
>
> The boys, neat in new grey suits and F.C. felt hats, will leave Southampton today in the *Caernarvon Castle*.
>
> Like all the others, Brian has been chosen from a family who, through bereavement or financial circumstances, cannot give him such opportunities in life.
>
> His father, sad yet satisfied, told me, "I know my boy will get the chances I could never give him under this marvellous scheme."
>
> The youngest in the party are two eight year olds. A ten year old who wants to be an architect is Tommy, who lost his mother when he was two and has since been cared for by his grandparents. Another Londoner is Geoffrey, of Curzon Street.
>
> The boys are the first batch of 700 who will eventually be students at the College.

The *Caernarvon Castle* was still rigged out as a troop ship. Two women, who stayed on as housemothers, accompanied the boys; one declared it was "a splendid sea trip", while the other said, "it was a long journey in those days and a terrible ship: they had not converted them from troopships, there were hammocks and primitive conditions". The eldest boy in the party added, "It was rather sad seeing these youngsters getting up to all the mischief on the ship going over, but every now and then getting homesick and crying for their people that they left behind." The sea journey ended at Cape Town and was followed by a three day train trip and then a journey by truck.

In the immediate years after the Second World War the white population in Rhodesia grew phenomenally. The white government there strongly encouraged white migration – child migration included – because it wanted to make a miniature South Africa, uniting and securing the mineral wealth of Southern and Northern Rhodesia. The Fairbridge Memorial College was opened in Rhodesia in 1946 and was to take some 300 children before it closed about ten years later. It was the last of the schools associated with Kingsley Fairbridge to be opened, but although Fairbridge's imperial dream was meant to start with a farm school in the Umtali (now Mutare) area of Southern Rhodesia, where his family home was, the British South Africa Company considered it was too young a country in which to start and refused to further the scheme.

Extraordinarily little is now on record about the Fairbridge scheme – it is as if it never existed. Its buildings are now mainly destroyed and it remains really only in the children's memories. The Fairbridge Society in London say they have no knowledge of it, indeed according to the wife of one of its longest-serving headmasters, the late Mr Robinson:

> When the school closed, London sent instructions that all files were to be destroyed. My husband was terribly upset and annoyed. A fortnight after he had done it, London wrote saying, "Could you tell us so and so?" and he had great glee in saying, "The files were destroyed on your orders." At first, when he took over, he allowed housemothers to read files and then he found the ones who were not suitable housemothers were making use of these files in a nasty way, so he withdrew all files from all staff.

It was in 1935 that it was first suggested that a Fairbridge school be established in Southern Rhodesia. The Fairbridge Society in London decided that as conditions for child migrants there would be so different from Australia, where its two farm schools then existed, the scheme should be carried out by a separate organisation. The Rhodesia Fairbridge Memorial College, based at Rhodesia House in London, was set up under the chairmanship of Lord de Saumarez and run by a London council. The aim of the school was laid down as pursuing "the Kingsley Fairbridge system of child emigration, the object of which was to fill the empty spaces of the Empire with selected children of sound stock from the over-crowded towns and cities of the United Kingdom".

The children were to join the white elite. The "College" would educate them so that they were qualified for a career "in agriculture, industry, mining or the public services". Farm labouring was out: "Rhodesian economic conditions . . . are effected [sic] by the presence of a large native population".

Ten years of discussions and delays (because of war) went by before Lord de Saumarez negotiated to buy a deserted RAF base at the foot of "Nthabas Induna" (the flat-topped Hill of the Chiefs), nine miles north-east of Bulawayo. The school opened there on 7 December 1946 with eighteen boys. One says he will never forget the grand reception they got at Bulawayo station when they arrived. The Mayor was there and the band was playing in the square. It was a welcome to the "Master Race".

According to the brochure, the children's background played a key part in their selection, in order that they should gain "access to the professions". They had to be healthy with "good natural intelligence" (back to the need for "sound stock"). The children themselves were very conscious of the IQ tests they had to pass at Rhodesia House. "Rhodesia has always been very selective about the people brought in," said one, who had been sent to Rhodesia at the age of eight. "One of the criteria is intelligence and social standing." Another said, "They wanted colonialists, albeit kids, but they wanted the right kind: they did not want the run-of-the-mill going out."

Maisie Wright, who was a psychiatric social worker in the Brighton region when the College started up, makes the point that much of the careful checking of the children's background was done by social workers like herself, all members of the British Federation of Social Workers (BFSW). They visited the homes of prospective child migrants and interviewed their relatives. Social workers became involved after news that a man representing the Fairbridge College was going around the schools in Brighton:

> He was desperate to get children. He was taking all the children he could and getting them out there. He did not mind who he got to go. Someone at the child guidance clinic described him as "a bouncy salesman" and we thought he went a bit over the top. The BFSW, which covered the whole country, heard about this and felt that not enough care was being taken about the background of these children and why they were being sent. The Brighton workhouse was called Warren Farm and the Brighton Education Committee did not want any of their girls to go. Why were these children being sent out like parcels?

The BFSW got in touch with the Memorial College and asked them to hand over any applications so that they could then send them through to the nearest social worker, who would visit the home, assess the situation and ask why the parent or guardian wanted to send the child(ren). "The forms the college sent out did not ask for the reason for the application," says Miss Wright. She found that because this "salesman" went round to the schools:

> A lot of ignorant people, who were very careless about their children, applied. I would say, "Do you realise you are sending these children away for good and you may never see them again?" and they would look surprised. I asked one woman in Brighton if she knew where Rhodesia was and she said, "Oh, yes, the other side of Haywards Heath" [some miles from Brighton]. If I saw anything like a decent home, I recommended that they were not sent.

One of her reports read:

> The mother seems to be an unselfish woman who is willing to relinquish her son. Seems genuinely fond of the boy and seems to be making this application mainly for consideration of his welfare. Paints a glowing picture of his character.

The application form's instructions from the London Council of Fairbridge to the parent or guardian were precise:

> On receipt of these forms arrangements will be made for a member of the BFSW to call at your home and interview you. Arrangements will also be made for an intelligence test of the child to be carried out. If the forms and report are satisfactory, you will be invited to bring the child to London for interview by our selection committee.

Maisie Wright often took the children up to the interview. "They would be told, 'You will be able to go to university, will be able to get a Rhodes scholarship to Oxford.' It's true, they were eligible, but none of them would get anywhere near that. They were rather grand people on the Committee. Some of them had not much idea of the background of these children. One man gave a talk about how the children could play polo and they showed not a glimmer of interest and did not even know what he was talking about." At these interviews, the Committee satisfied itself that the child was likely to benefit from the scheme and that the parent or guardian fully understood the conditions.

But the intervention of the BFSW was timely, as its news-sheet dated Jan-March 1947 shows:

> In cooperation with the promoters of this [Fairbridge] scheme, members of the Federation have stressed that emigration was suitable for carefully selected children who had not a normal home background and for whom a chance in a new environment might be beneficial. They felt it was not a project for boys who had opportunities of making good in this country and who had not suffered the loss of a good home.

Now we find this idea has triumphed at Rhodesia House. Selection is slower and more careful. Passages are not now booked in advance of selection and by a recent decision, parents who are able to provide satisfactorily for their children are not to be encouraged to send them abroad.

The selection panel now meets for examination of reports and to shortlist the children. There is an interval of two weeks for further enquiry and then the children and their parents or guardians are interviewed.

Miss Wright interviewed some one hundred children, though to the children themselves Rhodesia didn't mean much:

> They all had such terribly unsettled lives that one more move did not make much difference. To be going on a ship on the sea was exciting, but they wouldn't know how long it was going to take. Children did not ask questions in those days, did not say, "Will I get any pocket money?"

She took a great interest in them, later writing to the College for reports on how the children were getting on. Some must have given her pleasure, but not all: "A very likeable boy, developed well physically, excels in sport generally, scholastically well below average"; "A sound lad, but gives up the struggle far too easily"; "Improved, but is a whiner and has very little go except on sports field."

Sending children to Africa was sending them into a very different culture, more alien than Canada or Australia. None of the children had even seen an African, and aged six or seven, the children had no idea of the history of the place. They knew nothing of racial prejudice but their attitudes were naturally moulded as children:

> We were told that if we did not work hard, the black children would do so and get the jobs. In your late teens you start to think about these things and my views were influenced by the people around me.

Funding coming from the London Council for upkeep of the school turned out to be sporadic. "It was called the Rhodesia Fairbridge Memorial College to give it a grand name and improve the situation as far as applicants were concerned," said one of the migrants in the first group to go out in 1946. Indeed, the "College" was no more than a collection of RAF Nissen huts, with some good sports facilities, such as a swimming pool, that the airforce had put in. One boy's first impressions were that:

> The entire complex was of corrugated iron, clad with board on the inside. All the buildings were mounted on brick piers to protect them

from the rot and the white ants. Two of the parachute training rooms had been turned into classrooms. But despite the lack of privacy in dormitories, we grew to accept it.

Everyone was very conscious of costs. One of the early house-mothers said, "To begin with, we were terribly poor. England dressed the children for a year and paid the fare out. And then we became so poor that the Rhodesian government took us over and the children became wards of the state." The then Prime Minister of Southern Rhodesia, Sir Godfrey Huggins, was the man who backed this idea. Mrs Robinson confirmed that when her husband was appointed headmaster in 1948, his salary was paid by the Southern Rhodesian government, as the Council couldn't afford it.

To be quite honest the children were fed better. They were filled with bread towards the end of the London Council's rule. The only money my husband got out of Fairbridge was £7. 10s. 0d. a month for holiday duties, when the children did not go away. He was never off duty.

Nevertheless, as an ex-member of staff pointed out:

The Council spend money on sending General Hawthorn [the General Secretary] out every year and he had not a clue. We called him "the bloody general", and he would stay for five or six weeks and go round the junior dormitories; not the senior, he couldn't cope with the seniors.

One of the ex-juniors remembered these visits of Hawthorn's more affectionately:

Being an ex-general, he told us anecdotes and thought every child should know about Rudyard Kipling. And he would talk about elephants and tigers. He always made a custom of sitting there in the evening reading each dormitory a story.

The London Council continued to think of the Fairbridge children as the elite. One boy remembered hearing a visiting member from the Council saying at a Fairbridge cricket match, where a boy's shirt-tails had come out: "Don't you think we should keep the tone of our establishment up and get that young man to put his coat tails in." But at the same time Mr and Mrs Robinson were anxious to create at least a sense of family for the children ("The youngest we had came when he was four. We couldn't understand anyone parting with him"); their own children, born there, were brought up with the rest.

We had carol concerts at Christmas and we had a choir the first year which had all four parts, base, tenor, girls and juniors. There was an African flavour to Christmas, with dancing. We used to have a party for the children, with entertainment and crackers. Lunch was in the dining room, with all the trimmings. All had Christmas presents, paid for by the staff: they also had a birthday card each.

The boys had their own dens in the bush – one was built into an ant hill – and we used to go and visit them and they would give us "tea" when we got there. I remember one boy rushing up saying, "Mr Robbie, Mr Robbie, I have set the hayrick on fire."

My husband encouraged me not to be a mother, but to take a mother's view and help them as much as I could. The housemothers were supposed to be trained when they came out – and some of them were. Some of them coped better than others. The situation was difficult for every child: being taken from where you were established and being sent to somewhere completely strange, a whole new life. And he may have little quirks, like wetting the bed, and it becomes fear. He is frightened to tell anybody, frightened to tell the matron. And there were cases where it was found out and instead of being the mother, she became the matron and came down on the guy, which did not help.

The children sent to Fairbridge were fortunate in having Mr and Mrs Robinson in charge. Mr Robinson was regarded as stern but just and most ended up being happy there which was fortunate in view of the lack of concern from the British side.

Being the first, we soon got to know the place. We had a damn fine life there, no problems. We were allowed a great amount of freedom and were encouraged to camp out in the surrounding bush. Meat, eggs, vegetables were provided and we grew to love the wide open spaces. Local schools were fanatical about sport and it did not take much time for us to catch the bug: boxing, tennis, squash, cricket, rugby, soccer, swimming, basketball and athletics.   *Tom Paine*

We grew up in a bush atmosphere and a lot were more conversant with the bush than most Rhodesians. Every weekend we used to pack our bag and go to the bush, it was just magic. Snakes, wild cats. I had one cat giving birth in my bed. It probably made us more Africa. I love Africa today, waking up in the morning and listening to the birds, like the Crested Barbet. Maybe if I still lived in Glasgow, I would be bloody lucky if I recognised a pigeon or sparrow.   *George Stuart*

Everyone attended morning service in the chapel. I was a choir boy through to about fourteen. I have beautiful memories of evensong, partly because of the singing and also because it was a nice chance to meet the girls.   *Mike Wilkins*

Some children did have difficulties in settling down.

The sense of distance only came to me in the first few weeks. I said, "I want to go home now," and I found I couldn't. I was told it was too far. I was cushioned from that because my brother, four years younger, was due to come out and I was waiting for this. But the night before he was due to catch the train, the blanket he was wrapped in before the fire caught alight and he was in hospital for two to three years. I went to look for my brother and he wasn't there with the rest. It was two to three weeks after that I found out – letters took the same time to arrive as children – and I remember going through a pretty sad period then.

When we arrived, I got chickenpox and went straight into "hospital" at Fairbridge for fourteen days. And everyone else was sorted out and when I came out I was a stranger. I felt alone. There was nothing like counselling, the kind of counselling to get into the mind and into the heart and find out, "What is this kid thinking?" One just battled on through and had to make the best of it. I enjoyed school holidays because I went to a ranch and could go in the bush on my own.

The ranch referred to was part of a holiday scheme organised by the headmaster. As well as bringing in Rhodesian children to the school to board, he arranged for as many children as possible to stay with Rhodesian families in the holidays so that they could get to know Rhodesia and Rhodesian homes. If they were lucky, they went back to the same home time and time again, half adopted. At least most had a change and got away from the institution.

At school holidays we children went out and stayed with people and sometimes got very close to them: they became like second parents. For those who did not have someone like that, Fairbridge was an institution. It wasn't a home, despite the efforts of old man Robinson and some of the housemothers.

I had friends [Rhodesian boys] and I would go with them for the weekend, but not for a holiday. You would be selected to go for a holiday; they would say, "These people want two chaps, you two go." I was never selected. If, in their view, you are going to be a risk, to give the school a bad name, they wouldn't choose you. In their view, I was a bad egg because I was always in trouble.

At holiday time and Christmas time, they tried to get you to go to people, to anyone with a farm; but if you did not go, a lot felt it was a stigma. They got very withdrawn and it took quite a while to get them to join in something. We'd say, "Tonight we are going to go across the railway line" and these guys would sit there, morose, and just say, "Why has X gone, or Y gone?" Mr and Mrs Robbie tried to get you out and I went quite a few times. But the place got bigger and bigger and everyone had to have a turn.

Many in the first group of boys had been scouts and the scout mentality of inventiveness and team spirit prevailed. Above all, though, the boys believed that Fairbridge had made them into survivors and they constantly emphasise this:

The Fairbridge boys tended to become more individual, to do their own thing. You would find a group of four kids, twelve year olds, trekking, walking four to five miles into the bush. It made you tough and rugged. We made some damn good mates. A few of the kids couldn't take the pace and for one reason or another were sent back. Psychologically, some kids can't do it. Homesick, couldn't keep it up, didn't have the backbone. It wasn't a bed of roses.

What Fairbridge did do, it built in a hell of a lot of independence in people. We were encouraged to be independent, here it is, go for it. You did not ask, you went and got it. If you got thrashed you showed no pain because the rest of the prep room sat there and watched you . . . initially the girls were probably not as good at coping. We were in Africa, a man must be a man, playing cricket and water polo. I would never have seen a game of cricket if I had not gone. The teachers and the housemothers were brought out from England, all bloody fine people. Molly Cargill, our housemother, never said "Stop the fight", but came wading in from her room with a pillow and used to beat the hell out of us.

The experience of my youth taught me many things, most of all camaraderie and also I think self-sufficiency. I think most Fairbridge boys and girls were survivors. I don't know defeat; I don't lose; I only win. The day I met my [second] wife, she walked into the office and I said, "You are my next wife."

We used to make wine out of bananas, mulberries and so on. We used to climb up to the rafters where we'd keep bottles and fill them with sugar and yeast and put in marula fruit, paw paws, and marulas ferment and we used to bottle these things and forget about them and you could be lying on your bed having your after-lunch rest hour and these explosions would start and all this grog used to drip through the roof – which was damn nearly porous – and on to the floor.

We would have a bioscope [film show] on Saturdays in the scout hall. We had our own scout troop. On Sunday evening at 8.30 they used to have the hits of the week, like the latest South African record, and we all used to go into our housemother's room and have biscuits and coffee. It was a real thrill.

All the boys went to junior school at Fairbridge until the age of twelve, then transferred to local senior schools until they reached sixteen. At sixteen, they were suddenly out of both school and Fairbridge. Life wasn't that easy despite the fact that they were white.

My biggest criticism of Fairbridge was that I don't think that when we left school we were given any guidance. Yet everyone who went to Fairbridge had a certain IQ, a certain standard of education. A lot, on leaving, wasted that potential. You were told, "You will do this, you will do that." In my case, the headmaster went round and said, "Five guys to join a shoe company, you, you, you, you and you." As you walk out of the gate, it's really, "So long it's been good to know you." I was fired from the shoe company after three months. I had a drinking problem, well an attitude rather than a problem, and nearly put myself into the machine because I had been drinking.

I roamed around for a while after that. I had a job at the Post Office, and then I went on the railways as a fireman for two years and from there I went back to the UK and joined the Scots Guards. Then I joined the army over here and went to Kenya, then got demobbed. I tried farming in East Africa, but was deported after a confrontation with the Kenyans after I fired 300 Africans from the job.

I came down to South Africa and did all sorts of things: insurance, gents outfitting, cabaret – being a magician, doing card tricks and so on – and modelling. I then joined a large company as salesman and in over eighteen years went from that to sales manager, branch manager and then sales director of one of their franchises.

When you left Fairbridge, you were given some money – £10 I think – and you went to a clothing company to buy a sports coat, tie and shirt. You'd get a train ticket if you were going by train, and that's how you went out into the world. And you either made it or did not.

In between jobs I have slept in toilets, trains. You don't have parents to go to and you don't like forcing yourself on people. There's no rush to get a job if you know you are going to be fed but in my situation you are out there with nowhere to go, and you have to make it with what you have got and find a room which doesn't cost you a lot of money. Every day you are knocking on doors, asking for a job. You can't have a couple of months' holiday.

The early talk about Rhodes Scholarships came to very little. A few boys managed to get to the University of Cape Town, but one said he was not sure how it had been worked, "it seemed to be that if they felt you had the intelligence and passed exams, then they would give you an opportunity to go to university, for which I am very grateful. They say the government here paid for that."

The other difficulties many faced on leaving Fairbridge was forming relationships. Almost all had at least one parent living and if they had stayed in Britain they could have seen them and had some idea of the ups and downs of family relationships.

My wife was an only child and she had a lot of love. If her parents rowed, they made it up. If I shout at her, afterwards she knows what to do in that situation. But what do I do? Do I ignore it and build it up inside me? In effect, I tend to just switch off.

Another admitted that for many years he had a mother complex:

I was always involved with older women. I wanted to be mothered. When you get older you look at that. Once I had identified that and accepted maybe that is the cause, my attitude to it changed. I think I was a bit of a bastard to women: very selfish and cocksure and self-opinionated. It was probably my way of getting back at my mother, because I resented my mother for many years.

Other children had also not come to terms with their parent(s) sending them so far away. In any case, family relationships could not survive such a lengthy parting.

My father came to see me off when I left England and that was it. He gave me a watch, which I overwound on the first night. I would say I did not feel anything. It was something that was happening and I did it. When they told me at Fairbridge that my father had died, I did not feel anything at all, which was rather terrible.

When I went to Fairbridge, when I was seven, my mother couldn't tell me the truth, couldn't tell me why I was going. I suppose the reason was she felt unable to support both myself and my sister, but I resented my mother for years. When I was nineteen I went back to Scotland and saw her briefly. I did not remind her that I never knew why I had to go to Rhodesia. I think she was sorry because I was her first born and the hard times had gone and maybe she thought, "I could have got through it. And the price I paid is that I have lost my son."

After three or four years, my parents said they were happy to have us back and my two brothers returned. But my own feeling is that my brothers had difficulty integrating into the family. When I go back, I look them up; we don't write to each other.

As for myself, as a young man I never trusted anyone. My first relationship, with my wife at seventeen, was when I first did so. Before, it was dog eat dog and I was determined not to let myself be vulnerable to anyone.

Children damaged like this need professional help to cope with their feelings. One cottage mother at Fairbridge remembers taking three of the children in her dormitory to the psychiatrist at Bulawayo once a week. She couldn't recall just what he said to the children "but I do remember thinking what stupid questions they were". The school was to close in 1965, though last small parties of children came out in 1958. Mr and Mrs Robinson then went on some "after-care" tours:

> We went to see how the boys were getting on in their jobs. Quite a number were learner farmers and we went to see their bosses. But if they were going through a bad time, I don't think the guy would have admitted it. Every Christmas we would send a card with our address on it and in the New Year we would send a newsletter so they could keep a trace of those they were at school with. It has been very important.

Few of those sent out have returned to Britain. "The Rhodies" have all got a good standard of living, most having swimming pools, an attractive house and an acre or so of land. At the time of Ian Smith's unilateral declaration of independence (UDI), they fought against African independence and many went to live in South Africa. One Fairbridgean woman who stayed was on the verge of leaving for Britain when she was interviewed:

> I can't educate my daughter here, or get the books, newspapers or magazines I want. I'm going home for my daughter's sake. I still look on England as home. I am still a British citizen, I would never change my citizenship.

Currency restrictions are such that Zimbabweans cannot take more than a limited amount of money and property outside the country. And the exchange rate renders their pensions worthless. As one said, "If I end up returning to Britain without a cent, I'll sue the British government for sending me out in the first place." But few are thinking of returning, instead they still manage to maintain a white colonial life style, with black servants. Ask them if they would like to go back and they laugh at you. As one man said:

> If I'd stayed in England, I would have been somebody who worked in a station, sweeping up cigarette butts. But coming out to a country like Rhodesia, it's so fantastic from the point of view of the wide open spaces. If you go back to Britain you see all these little houses, one next door to the other: you haven't got the space and environment that we have here. It's a different way of life, free but easy. If you want to go

ranching or wild game safari, you do it. In England you are more restricted.

Fairbridge proved to be so good. We are proud of our achievements, to have done so darn well.

The Fairbridge children were sent out to be the white elite, and from that standpoint, the Fairbridge scheme, in what the whites once called Rhodesia, has been a complete success. But those who want to leave and re-start their life in another country must do so from scratch. They were sent out without choice from Britain, with the aid of the government. If any should choose to come back, the government should be equally prepared to help them.

9

Australia: The Lost Souls

So few people in Britain know that children were still being sent to Australia until the mid-1960s that one man, compulsorily detained in a UK psychiatric hospital, had his claim of being shipped to Australia as a child dismissed for years as part of his delusion. But after the Second World War, the main child migrant agencies, in a burst of vigour, packed off some 10,000 British children to Australia, treating it virtually as a dumping ground. As one nine year old remembered, "They sent a double-barrel from certain homes. But they only ever sent the one lot from the Middlesbrough Home, where I was. So we reckoned it was, you know, get rid of the *riff-raff*."

John McGillion, who came from a Northern Ireland children's Home, said that he and the rest were never asked if they wanted to go to Australia: "We were told we were going on a holiday. But that holiday never ended." He well remembers the vast numbers who went:

Oh, we were literally hundreds on the boat. There were British, Irish, Scottish, Welsh. The ship went from place to place, just picking up children. It was a possibility there could have been at least eight or nine hundred on that ship; and there were also two or three more ships that arrived at Fremantle with hundreds of other boys. We all stepped down that gangplank like sheep. And we were actually sorted out like sheep. Each individual boy was sort of separated from one side to the other, as if to say, you go that way and you go that way. And that's how some of my mates that were in Derry with me did not go to the same orphanage as me.

An eleven-year-old girl, who was also brought up in a Catholic orphanage, remembers how she joined the exodus:

I was lying in bed and the nun who was sitting on one of the beds looked up at me and said, "How would you like to go to Australia?" And I was reading a *National Geographic* and I thought, well, maybe she thinks I'm reading about it. And I said, "I never gave it a thought."

"Oh," she said. "Think about it." The next morning we all met in the washroom and I said to one of the girls, "Sister so-and-so asked me if I wanted to go to Australia." And she said, "She asked me too!" Another girl said, "Yeah, she asked me as well." And apparently they'd dotted it around. We didn't even know how far away it was, or how big the country was. We didn't know where we were going.

The history of child migration in Australia is in many ways a history of cruelty, lies and deceit. For instance, children were told that their parents were dead; that they came from deprived backgrounds; that they had been "rescued" and should be grateful. As one who was eight when she was sent out to Australia said:

You felt you were nothing, you just didn't have any self-worth at all. The nuns were always telling us we were found in the gutter and they'd given their lives up to look after us. I wish they hadn't, I might have had more freedom in the gutter. I used to think, how could they say things like that? They don't know where half of us come from.

Yet these children were not orphans. And most of the families they came from were not poor or deprived. Marriage breakdown and illegitimacy rose sharply during and after the Second World War and unwanted children were often placed in children's Homes in the understanding that they would be fostered or adopted. This belief stopped the parent(s) and other family members from enquiring about the children. One woman, sent to Australia at the age of four, said:

I subsequently found out from my aunt that neither my mother, aunts or uncles knew that I had gone to Australia. They had been told I was adopted in Ireland and although they had wondered about me and wanted to see me, they did not want to interfere. My aunt and uncle were shocked to hear I had been shipped to Australia.

Many children had genuinely been adopted in the United Kingdom but their adoptions had subsequently broken down. They had been returned to the adoption agency, and promptly dispatched to Australia. The adoption order was ignored and the natural parents were never told and were totally unaware that their child was suddenly thousands of miles away. One couple were actually half way through adoption proceedings, only to find that the eight-year-old girl in question had been whisked off to Australia. One boy, whose parents were divorced and whose father had custody of him and his younger brother and sister, was taken into care by the child welfare when his father seemed unable to cope. He went from one children's Home to another throughout England. He was a bright boy, coming top in the mock eleven plus exams at his local primary school and was looking forward to going on to grammar school. Then suddenly he and his brother and sister were shipped off to Australia and the Fairbridge Farm at Molong in New South Wales.

Many parents – particularly single women – who were in temporary difficulties after the war were persuaded by church or charitable agencies to send their child to Australia. Many went on to marry and successfully bring up more children. The one in Australia was lost or forgotten. One child who came out to Australia in 1947, said, looking back:

> When I was young I used to feel *bugger* my mother, she dumped me, I don't want to know her. But she must have felt so guilty when she had me. She was unmarried, a Catholic in Northern Ireland, she must have been under terrible pressure. I should think, from what I now know of my gran, that she said to her, "You won't enter my house again ever if you keep the babe."

Children who were sent to Australia with brothers and sisters were also promised they would all be kept together. Yet often they were split up on arrival and either never saw their brothers and sisters again, or too rarely to have a normal brother and sister relationship. George Wilkins, for instance, segregated from his sister who had bad health and poor eyesight, under the single-sex cottage scheme at Fairbridge Farm School in Molong, remembered "Life was very bad for my sister. She was the target for being picked on, abused by both the other kids and the staff. She got beaten badly."

The children would write letters to friends left behind in the children's Home in England or even to a parent or relation, if they knew one. But if they wrote anything critical they got a beating and the letter was never sent. "We had to say how wonderful everything was," said one girl. This passivity and acceptance of their lot remained with the children into adulthood, so that only as one or two have dared tell their story did others start to confirm it, to admit that, yes, it had happened to them too. It was a cathartic moment for many.

The policy of the agencies was to cut children off from their previous life, in order to make it "easier" for them to adjust to their new country. It often happened that members of a family unsuccessfully tried to stop children from being sent to Australia and offered to take them in themselves, but were rejected. Those who asked the agencies about the welfare and whereabouts of the children were misled or refused information.

The children, afraid and insecure at their sudden transportation, lost even more confidence in their early days in Australia. One girl remembers the nuns in the orphanage calling them "those dreadful English girls". Another can't forget an immigration officer shouting "British scum" at her. This excerpt from a report by a Fairbridge representative to the Society's headquarters in London about a party of children who arrived in Australia on 19 May 1950 to go to a Fairbridge farm school, shockingly underlines the attitude towards them. George Wilkins came across this report years later, and it is easy to imagine his feelings as one of the group:

This party is the worst which we have ever received. From whichever aspect they are considered, there is nothing to recommend them . . . My immediate reaction to their appearance was unfavourable. They were unattractive, sullen in their demeanour and quite different from the cheery children we used to receive. I made contact immediately with the conducting officers and their report was most adverse . . .

Before selection for such a chance in life I think children should have their intelligence quotient assessed and also as far as possible, hereditary and emotional tendencies reviewed . . .

The Immigration Medical Officer told me after the examination of the children that from his point of view they were the worst party he had seen and he expressed considerable surprise that the majority of them had been passed as suitable immigrants . . . his oral report to me in X's case [name withheld] was that she was definitely dull and might be found on the psychiatric examination to be held next Friday to be sub-normal . . . She has a squint . . . she is certainly the worst from a medical point of view . . .

Fairbridge cannot afford to handle children of the type comprising the "Largs Bay" party. Such children created a thoroughly bad impression on the voyage out and it is impossible to prevent such impressions being broadcast . . . We may be able to do something with the younger children in the party, but personally I wrote off the older ones as being anything in the way of a credit to Fairbridge . . .

We have in the past featured that it is an advantage to Australia to have immigrants of good sound British stock. If they are neither good nor sound we must modify our statements and lose one of our most profitable items of propaganda.

The children sent to Australia had practically no chance of being adopted or fostered on arrival. They were all sent out to orphanages, farm schools or institutions of some kind or another, despite not being orphans as so many were led to believe. One report in an Australian paper about the number of Australians eager to adopt the eighty British girls arriving at the Catholic-run Goodwood

Orphanage, quoted this reply from the Catholic Social Service Bureau:

> In this instance the Catholic Church had no intention of making them available for adoption.
> The children would be reared at the institution under the care of the Catholic Church until placed in employment under supervision.
> The children were settling in to their new home. Their only complaint was that they found it difficult to become accustomed to the heat.

Their only complaint? To outsiders, Goodwood looks a fine building, with a large courtyard planted with trees and colonnades which provide shade from the sun. But many small British girls who came out to this orphanage after the war describe their childhood there in heartbreaking terms.

It was the Catholic boys who were subject to far more abuse. They were sent to the Christian Brothers' isolated farm schools of Bindoon, Tardun and Clontarf, in Western Australia, and faced a regime of brutalising cruelty. Only in the brochures and money appeals did these places sound inviting. In a section on Bindoon, for example, which stresses the Christian Brothers' efforts "to uplift poor boys and give them equal opportunities with the more fortunate sons of comfortably-circumstanced parents", there is a glowing description of the terrain: "Such surroundings cannot fail to instil into the youthful mind a love for his environment and occupations." But the reality was harshly different. To one English boy, Bindoon – some 60 miles north of Perth – seemed like the back of beyond:

> It was like going into a place where there's no houses and absolutely nothing. Just trees! And it was totally different surroundings. We'd never seen trees about fifty, sixty and a hundred feet high. And it just looked like a jungle to us, especially in the darkness in a country where we'd never been before. We didn't know where the heck we were going. I know for a fact we were very frightened for the first few days we were there, right out in the heart of the bush. I know that quite a few of the boys done a bunk.
> Many feel bitter about being sent there without being aware of what was happening. It was very harsh, you had to cope or you had a breakdown.

Bindoon was enormous – 17,000 acres. Now, as you walk down the red, dusty drive for some two miles, past the fourteen Stations of the Cross, and see the vast, ornate buildings of the orphanage (rather like unexpectedly coming across St Paul's in the desert), it is almost impossible to realise that the first child migrants built it *all* from scratch. As John McGillion says:

> There was only two small buildings when we went there. We used to pick up the rocks from the paddocks and put them into big heaps. We cleared quite a lot of the land there. We'd push all the timber into a big bundle and put a match to it.
>
> I remember one ten ton pick-up truck. The Brother said, "You boys load it up and I'll unload it." We thought it would be fun to see him unload the sand on his own! I'd never seen a pick-up truck in my life before. There was a lot of work involved in the place, a lot of physical labour.
>
> My main job there was making the bricks for the building by hand, mixing the sand and cement. We had a machine that used to press the shape of the brick. The head Brother used to sit there and watch me making the bricks and then he'd have his cup of tea in the morning. And sometimes I used to get wild, and he'd leave his cup and saucer and his little plate, and I used to break them and put them in the bricks. It was unfortunate that it happened that one of the bricks broke while he was there and he spotted half a saucer inside the brick. I don't think he took kindly to it. I got the brick put on the plate for my dinner with the half a saucer sticking out of it!

Another boy at Bindoon never forgot the "disgusting job of cleaning out sewage pits" and being told that they could build themselves a swimming pool. "We all worked really hard on construction only to discover that it was a dam for the orchards. I remember the orchards at the Home although we never saw a piece of fruit. I remember often having no shoes, although my oldest sister tells me that money was sent for shoes."

The boys often foraged for their own food. As one said:

> We would get porridge in the mornings, and a cup of tea; at lunch we'd get toast. And then for dinner we might get rabbit. We'd go out and trap them with rabbit traps or we'd literally dig them out of the ground. We'd take a big bag and dig deep.

Another said that he could never remember having enough to eat and was always hungry:

> Although we worked like slaves all day, I cannot remember having lunch. I do remember breakfast and tea – bread and milk, which we called SLOPS. Sometimes we used to have cabbage soup – a lot better than SLOPS. I also remember pinching the stale bread out of the pigs' food before it was all mixed to mash.

Sometimes the boys were given sago and one recalled how he could never eat it. "I would dry retch and you were not allowed to leave the table until it was finished. And we used to make up jock straps and put the sago in there and hope you did not get caught." Many of the Christian Brothers at Bindoon paid no regard to the children's welfare, hitting them on any occasion and with no regard for the consequences. One remembered that his first day at Bindoon, aged twelve, "started with Brother Keaney hitting me on my head with his walking stick".

> I was also hit across the face by [another Brother], who knocked me from one side of the room to the other. On one occasion I saw a Brother hit a boy on his knee with a stick even though his knee was inflamed. Another case was a boy working on terrazzo who broke a slab when he was taking it out of the mould. He got the strap for days after finishing work, by Brother Keaney. Another boy, when caught after escaping, was dipped head first in a forty-four gallon drum of liquid lime.

John McGillion was on some scaffolding one day, about fifteen to twenty feet up, when, he said:

> I was literally pushed off by one of the Brothers who gave me a backhander and I fell down on to a concrete ledge. I slipped just about every disk in my back. I did get up and I was half way up to where we were going for meals and I just collapsed. I was picked up and put into a special room called the sick room and when I didn't get any better, I was taken down to Royal Perth Hospital. And I had to stay in bed with weights on my legs. I thought I'd never walk again, but I managed to.

The Brother who did this never came to see John in hospital, even though he spent months there. Nor did any other of the Brothers. John still makes excuses for them. "I suppose they didn't have the time," he said. And of the Brother who originally hit him: "I don't think that was done deliberately, I wouldn't like to say it was." He went on calmly to talk of other "accidents", all of which he said "were nothing to talk about, really":

> One boy lost his eye, through another accident; and there was another one, well that was his own fault. He'd run away to a holiday resort and a truck [collecting him] got bogged and the truck ran over him, ran over his leg. But it was carelessness on his part, it wasn't actually the Brothers' fault. It was lucky it was only on sand.

The children had no option other than to accept what happened. Only in later years did they reassess and become angry. Violet Davis, for instance, who was at Fairbridge Farm at Pinjarra and went into Pinjarra hospital for an operation, had ether spilt into her eye while there, which blinded it. "I remember them, from Fairbridge, sitting on the bed, but no help was offered, no compensation. It went down in the records as being hereditary. I am disgusted at there being no compensation."

Persistent cruelty was not confined to Bindoon. Colin Reidy, who went to Clontarf Orphanage from the nearby junior school at Castledare – which he had enjoyed – said:

I went to Clontarf when I was about twelve and that's when the brutality started. Maybe it was because I was headstrong. There was this attitude by the Brothers to overpower and I wasn't averse to answering back at first. Then you withdraw within yourself and they take that as a sign of weakness and they've got to belt this weakness out of you. There were only two or three of us in my age-group that did not end up in psychiatric Homes or in jails.

I was never terribly quick at school and this Brother would stand at the back of my desk and I would be writing and if I did not cross a "t" or dot an "i", I would get the strap on the back of my head.

You became very wise very young: you learned to satisfy the sadistic instincts of the Brothers. If you did not cry you would cop it on the other hand and then on the back of the hand, so as soon as you got the first cuts you would start crying. But then they became wise and they twigged that and so never took any notice. They would put your hand on the table so the full impact was there and you couldn't drop your hand.

They seemed to pick out a few kids and I was one. The amount of work you had to do before you got something to eat was enormous and in those days they were embarking on extensive modernisation of Clontarf which we were required to do. I can vividly recall the skin being sheered off my hands hauling sugar bags full of soil. You would have to walk 300 or 400 yards to dump the soil, clay earth, in the sugar bags for nine or ten hours every day. If you did not shift a certain amount of soil each day, you did not get tea and you knew then you were singled out for the rough treatment. And it was, "Reidy, go and pick up the bags and wash them." And there were 140 or 150 and you would be washing them till nine at night.

I became fairly good at sport and the Brothers were sports mad and once in the quadrangle one said, "You reckon you are good at the boxing? Let's see you." And he got this other unbeatable boy and every time this boy knocked me down, the Brother would get you and stand you up again.

The Christian Brothers had a physical cult. They encouraged competition in sport but this inevitably generated more violence: the boys went out to kill.

The worst incident in Colin's account was when he was caught sharing his bread with a very sickly boy:

I got this almighty whack with a strap on the side of my face. I think that's when I broke and I got the knife and rammed it in the Brother's

stomach. But he was wearing a cassock. The school got into an uproar
and this Brother had me on the wall and was hitting me, bang, bang,
with his fist and the next moment the kids jumped on him *en masse*:
they had had enough.

I ran away that night and got half a mile down the road and along
comes a Brother on a horse and picked me up. I was put into a cold
shower and flogged for three hours.

One ex-Christian Brother, who spent some years at Bindoon
and saved at least three from drowning in the swimming hole,
wrote to one of those he had saved after seeing him on television
talking about his experiences. He admitted that, looking back, it
might have been a blessing if the creek had claimed them, in view
of what a terrible life many ultimately led, "suicides, alcohol,
broken marriages, loneliness, desertions – a life of misery".

Some of the sexual abuse of children that took place in the
orphanages run by the Christian Brothers was criminal (see Nigel
Fitzgibbon's account in Chapter 2). At least half a dozen boys had
to have corrective surgery. Yet none of the doctors involved
reported these cases, nor did they report the general injuries that
took place under suspicious circumstances and placed boys in
hospitals. As one boy said, "For so long nobody would listen to us.
We were getting farmed out to families at holidays and we told
them these things and they wouldn't believe it." Those Christian
Brothers who were not involved in sexual abuse also turned a
blind eye. Colin Reidy recalls that:

The Brothers often came to the bed and pulled your clothes back and
tried to fondle you and that was one of the reasons I was singled out
because I wouldn't take it: I would kick and spit. They would ask
questions like have you learned to ejaculate? Because I flatly refused to
go along with it, I knew I was in a lot of trouble, so I would rush down
at eleven at night to the priest and wake him up and talk to him and he
kept promising he would do something about it, but he never did.

Some have found it easier to blank out what happened. Asked if
he had ever been sexually abused, one man said, "I never actually
experienced it but I believe it did happen. I'm not saying, exactly,
that it is true, or it isn't. Well, I wouldn't say it didn't happen and I
wouldn't say it did happen. But I believe it did, at some stage it did
happen."

If children are cruelly treated and constantly criticised, in the
end, like battered wives, they believe it must be their own fault.
They need help to accept that the way they were treated was
deliberately cruel, that they were not to blame. Boys were accused
of masturbation, "detected" by not going to mass or communion.

They were pressured into admitting things they had not done so as not to be beaten. This kind of psychological pressure was immense. One Clontarf boy, later to become a priest himself, remembers having to assemble in hall every Saturday morning, 150 boys on each side:

> The Brother would look up and down every row and every person had to watch and when your eyes met he would nod, that meant you had to go out front. You tried to think what you had done. You would be stripped naked and beaten but first you had to tell everyone why you were there. But you didn't know why you were there.

There were the children who cried in bed at night, afraid to wake up the next morning. And there were children who no longer cried. Some, reacting to the cruelty inflicted on them, would in turn inflict their anger on smaller boys by beating them, or they would be cruel to animals. There was a place at Clontarf nicknamed "Cat Island" where many of the children crucified cats.

The boys sent out to farm schools run by other agencies met less systematic cruelty. One boy, for instance, sent out to the Fairbridge Farm School at Pinjarra, some thirty miles from Perth, says that life there was hard, even harsh, but fair. Another, sent to Molong, an isolated farm about 200 miles from Sydney, says that though he himself was not treated badly there, he deeply resents the treatment meted out to some of the other children. He feels many there were deeply unhappy, leading at its most extreme, he believed, to suicide:

> One boy had gone into hospital to have his tonsils out. Instead of coming back to Molong, he ran away. There was a full-scale search and he broke into a farm truck, took a .22 rifle, and shot himself. It was hushed up. It was said he was suffering from a post-operative problem. It was really because he had run away and was being hunted like an animal.

Although discipline was tough at the Fairbridge farm schools, like Canada the quality of life depended crucially on which "cottage" a child was allocated to, as some of the cottage "mothers" were quite unsuited to look after children. George Wilkins, who managed to keep out of trouble and was seldom caned, says he remembers it as being a place "totally without love":

> It would have been nice one day in all those years to have had a friendly arm on the shoulder, but never even once did that happen. I feel I totally turned off personally. People say to me, "Weren't there

any good times?" But I really don't remember any good times except perhaps when I wandered off by myself across the paddock.

A nine year old boy, one of the 3,000 or so sent out by Barnardo's, went to Greenwood, a Barnardo home in Sydney which opened in 1951, and said the treatment was strict, "but I enjoyed it. We went to local primary schools, were well looked after and well fed." Those who went to the Barnardo farm school at Picton, in New South Wales, called the city kids "weaklings", and the city kids in turn admitted that "it was pretty tough work at Picton".

The girls sent out to Australia faced a bleak childhood, too. Again, the Roman Catholics had the worst of it. One girl had a particularly hard beating by a reverend mother, which affected her into adult life. It started one night in the dormitory after she had committed a misdemeanour earlier in the day.

The reverend mother came up with this huge strap off the belly of a carthorse. That's how thick and hard it was. She whacked me one right through the sheet and of course that hurt, so I jumped out the other side of the bed. And that made her mad, because she couldn't get at me. Anyway, she whacked and she lashed out, and sometimes she got me and sometimes she didn't. Meanwhile, the English kids were cheering me on.

She got so mad because this was going on that when she finally got me, she was in a fury. So much so that she ripped my nightie off, and there I was in the raw. And of course trying to cover myself up, she just got stuck into me. My body was just covered in welts, but apart from that hurting, I hurt *inside*. I had a series of hypnosis sessions with a doctor, about five years ago, and I think I got it out, because I could never ever talk about that, without absolutely going into tears something chronic.

I think they knew that the reverend mother had gone beyond what should have been done, because I then sat on the seat – in the yard they had seats under the veranda – and didn't speak to anybody for at least a week. I never went to church; I wouldn't go to the dining room. And one of the other nuns used to come over and bring me special cakes to try and get me out of it.

Anyway, a family that befriended us on the boat used to come up and see us. And this particular day I was still sitting on the bench and they wanted to know why I was sitting and they told him. And he came over to me and he was fuming! He said, "Show me those welts." And he saw them and he took his wife, walked straight out of the orphanage and straight to the archbishop and reported it. Now it never got into the papers. But the archbishop came to the orphanage and he told them the strap was never to be used again and someone else was put in charge there.

The readjustment to Goodwood Orphanage was traumatic enough for all the girls because they were still bewildered by their journey across the world.

To me it was such a feeling of loss. I thought, I'm never going to see England again. Because we'd been on the ship for so long, we knew it would take a long time to get back. And who was going to send us back? What chance did we have of going back? None.

Eleven year old

The nuns who were the Sisters of Mercy showed no mercy right from the word go. *Eleven year old*

When we first came out we all had this beautiful long hair and we all had to have it cut and it was just hacked off, mine was cut off with secateurs and it left so many sores on me head that I had to go into hospital. *Nine year old*

The girls were not allowed to keep any personal possessions. Anything they had when they arrived was taken away. Personal items like toothbrushes had to be shared – even their underclothes. One, sent out at the age of nine, remembers, "I had a doll, it had a green and white dress, it was my prize possession, the only thing I ever had and they took it away. I've never forgiven that nun for that."

Many say that one of the worst things at Goodwood Orphanage was that they received no care or kindness. As one girl said:

What I missed most was a bit of love. You had no one, you had the girls you come out with but they were in the same boat as you. Some of the nuns were nice, but still they didn't give you the love you needed. I think when someone's sick or going through an emotional thing they should be shown a bit of love, but you weren't. I think to bring up a child you've got to give them love so they have the security to go out into the world.

Such lack of love in childhood has inevitable repercussions in later life. One woman remembers that when she married and had a son of her own, she couldn't cuddle him.

I found it very hard to put my hands around him. If I give myself, I think, what's going to happen? There's something there: I can't do it. I can love my dog, and show affection to him, but with a human being it's different. I suppose it was what was lacking in childhood. Even today, when I see my son and I'm standing there, I still find it hard to bring my hands up to him. I still don't squeeze him.

Tensions at Goodwood were increased by the fact that there were also Australian girls at the orphanage, who were favoured and were visited by their parents.

We used to fight because we weren't going to be friendly with the Australian girls. They were alien to us. I can't remember becoming friendly with any of them.   *Twelve year old*

Dorothy Chernikov, who arrived at Goodwood when she was twelve, wanted desperately to be accepted by the Australian girls:

I just wanted to *belong*. I felt very lonely. And I felt that none of the Aussies really liked us and the only way that they'd like us was to do the things they dared us to. For instance, the nuns were praying in the chapel and one of the Aussie kids would say, "I dare you to go up into the gallery and play the organ," because I was very musical. And I started "On top of Old Smokey" and that kind of thing. The nuns were furious and I was locked up in the attic from about five o'clock till about nine at night. But I didn't care. I thought, as soon as I get out of here, I'll be friends with the Aussies. I got the strap lots of times: pulling a chair away from a nun, that was a dare, and that got me a real strapping. In the end, I started to be very friendly with most of them because they thought, she's a dare-devil.

Dorothy was one of the girls who could have been adopted in Australia. The first year she was there, she was allowed to go out on holiday to an Australian family, who became so fond of her they wanted to bring her up as their own daughter.

I was really hurt because I thought, Oh here I've got a mother! Here I've got a home to go to! They never liked taking me back to the orphanage. It was really sad. They even went up to the Archbishop. And nothing came of it. They went to loads of trouble trying to get me, but it was taboo.

It was the cruelty and the rigid discipline enforced at Goodwood that made so many of them hate their life there. Nita Brassy, who has been through extensive psychotherapy and hypnotherapy to try to help her overcome the deep depression she feels was caused by her childhood experiences, says:

For the slightest infraction of the rules they'd beat the hell out of you. I mean, if you were found with a hole in your sock they'd stick a needle through your heel. If you got your prayers wrong or your sums wrong, you were punished. And if you wet your bed you were made to stand up in front of the class with your wet sheet over you. That's no way to treat a lonely, insecure child.

A number of these frightened girls started to wet the bed. And Nita Brassy points out, there was no understanding of this, just severe punishment. As well as having to stand with their wet sheets on their heads, the girls were beaten:

> There were about seven in our dormitory that wet the bed and we were put in what was called the sleepout. And every night the head nun there used to come up and thrash us for wetting the bed. And I was terrified of going to sleep in case I wet the bed, but every morning I was wet again.
>
> It makes me feel sick, remembering it. We were put across the bed and our pants were pulled down and we were belted. We used to run our bums under hot water to make them swell up, hoping we'd have to go to the doctor's. It was a leather stick, about that thick [one inch] and that long [a foot and a half]. And they'd hit you on the top of your hands. And this one nun had a bamboo cane and she'd raise her hand so far back and, Oh! that was so painful.

> You'd get thrashed for *anything*! If you tore your dress or if your shoes were too worn out. So, you know, you got used to it. And you got frightened of it. It got to the stage that you were scared stiff to say anything out of place.

> For breakfast, you'd get half a cup of milk and you'd be lucky to get cornflakes. And afternoon teatime you'd come home from school and you'd get bread and jam. Later you'd get sausages and mash. I mean, you weren't fed that well. We thought, come to Australia and the food'll be terrific. But it wasn't. We just wondered what we'd copped.

> I didn't like the orphanage, I hated it, the nuns were cruel, they'd bloody belt you all the time. When I first came out here it was like coming to the Charles Dickens era. Those nuns were like Gestapo, it was like being in a prison. You used to be punished for the smallest thing. All they did was send you to church, punish you and make you pray.

> One nun there, she'd get you at the end of the week and she'd say, how many times did you go to Communion this week? And of course me being a lark, I said, oh, you know, I went every day. She'd say, "No, you didn't. You went five times." And as a punishment, she make us sit there. And she'd watch you. And if you blinked your eyes, you'd have to sit there for an extra half an hour.

One girl, who went to Goodwood early in 1951, remembered two of the nuns there treating the girls with great kindness. They both finally left to go to a different Order, because she thought, "they were pretty upset about some of the things that went on in the orphanage". But for the girls in Western Australia, there was little to choose between Goodwood, Nazareth House in Geraldton and St Joseph's Orphanage, in Subiaco, a suburb of Perth.

When they arrived in the huge dormitories of St Joseph's, there weren't enough beds and they had to sleep on the floor. A nine-year-old girl who went there said that the first day wasn't too bad, "But after that we had a rude awakening." They had to get up at five in the morning and get down on their hands and knees and polish:

We used all to be in a line with a rag and it was "One-Two-Three-MOVE." It was really very, very degrading. We had pyjamas that were inspected every morning and if they were slightly soiled we would get beaten. There were lovely bathrooms which were never used. On the veranda there used to be ten or a dozen buckets which you used to go to the toilet. And you'd be sitting on a bucket and the next ten girls would stand in front of you, waiting their turn.

As well as the unused bathrooms, the girls also had uniforms, which they were only allowed to wear in marching competitions. These quite often won the "best dressed" prize but as soon as the girls returned they'd have to take them off. Sadly, many recollections centre around the sadism of one particular nun. That nine year old remembers:

She would flog the living daylights out of us and I mean FLOG. We were beaten with bamboo sticks which had little bits of iron in, you know, where the bamboo joins. The leg of a wood chair would be used; our hair would be pulled; the belt would be used.

Sometimes if she was really mad we would go up to this beautiful block of bathrooms which had tiles on the floor and we would have to kneel there for maybe two days and two nights. There might be three of us in trouble. We weren't allowed to talk or anything.

Geraldton in those days was only a small place and the convent Home was effectively in the bush. Life there was spartan and hard, discipline was rigid; you'd get a clout or a beating if you disobeyed the nuns. The children were seldom taken out by the nuns but the place was too isolated for them to dare to go out on their own. "It felt like a prison," one said. "You weren't allowed out of the front gate and at night all the gates were locked. But we never really thought of running away because we knew we had nowhere to go." The repression matched that at the other girls' orphanages:

Even to have an argument with somebody was wrong ... we'd be punished if we had a fight with somebody. And if anyone did something wrong and didn't own up, we were all punished; we were made to walk around this courtyard for nearly an hour, until

somebody owned up and said they did something wrong. It was petty
little things like a cake missing off a plate. You know if children are
hungry, they'll eat a piece of cake, won't they. You do it at home and
nobody takes any notice of it.   *Eight year old*

Life was very regimented. "You felt you were never going to get
a break from this kind of life," said Denise Trowsdale, who was
eight when she went there:

Six o'clock we were up and sometimes quarter to six. We changed into
our dresses for mass; after mass we had to change into our overalls to
go to breakfast and do our chores.
   I worked in the chapel and so I had to sweep and dust the whole
chapel, put the vestments away and generally clean up. Then I'd
change into uniform for school, change out of our uniform to go to
lunch, after lunch do our chores. We had to do all our own washing
up, cleaning the tables and resetting. Then it was school, and mostly
we didn't get out of school until a quarter to four. Then we had to go
up to church and pray, that kept us till half past four, then most of us
went off to do our chores. I had to go to the chapel again, to clean up,
polish the floor after everybody had used it; and do all the lamps,
change the flowers, set up the vestments for the priest the next
morning. I still have scars on my knees from all the hours spent
kneeling on the floor and polishing.
   Saturday mornings, it was *work, work, work,* all morning. All the
chapel had to be waxed and polished. The verandas on either side were
wooden: they had to be waxed and polished as well. They were open
to the weather, so when it rained, all the wax was washed off.
Saturday afternoon was spent in the massive big laundry, with all this
industrial machinery. It took two of us to manage every machine. In
England, we would have been playing out in the warm sunshine,
enjoying ourselves. But here it was hard labour.

Everything revolved round the Church. Although this is a
natural focus in Catholic institutions, religion was emphasised far
more than the girls had been used to in England:

Sunday wasn't much fun, because as soon as we'd done our chores
there was choir practice, then we had to go to church for Rosary, and
then come down for lunch. Then there were a few hours in the
afternoon when we were free, and then we had to go to church again!

The boys in the orphanages never saw women. Any sexual
experience, through the Christian Brothers, was homosexual. It
resulted in many having difficulties in relating to women at all.
And because the nuns regarded sex as being unmentionable and
dirty, this had an immensely damaging effect on the girls too,
giving them a fear of sex and men. The girls were never taught

anything about sex except never to kiss with your mouth open and
to marry a good Roman Catholic boy. When they later went out
with men or married, their fears resurfaced and often destroyed
the relationship.

> I had a fantastic guilt complex about sex. My first marriage was
> hopeless, I was sexually frigid, I didn't know how to relate to men. I
> got married because I was pregnant. Quite a few of us girls got
> pregnant in our teens and had to marry. But as far as human
> relationships were concerned we had no experience whatsoever.
>
> When I left I remembered I met this guy and he kissed me. And I
> thought I was pregnant! Because I never ever heard anything about
> sex. It was a doctor who told me the facts of life. They used to show us
> films and if a lady was in trousers, or had something short on, or a
> tight frock, the nun used to put their hand over the lens, and say,
> "Can't watch that," and then have a further look and say, "No, can't
> watch that!" That's how strict it was. And we used to have to go on
> three days' retreat. We weren't allowed to talk for three days and we
> had to go in the chapel about five times a day and listen to stories
> about the devil and evil. Like tight clothing was a sin; prolonged
> kissing was a sin.

The nuns' attitudes also encouraged the girls to feel a great
shame about their bodies and their sexuality: for example, the girls
had to wear pants in the bath. When one girl's first period started,
she had no idea what the blood was and hid her pants behind the
door:

> I thought it was a catastrophe! I didn't know what it was, but did I get
> a belting for that; you know I felt I'd been stained or something. There
> were no sanitary pads, you only had old rags that you used to have to
> wash. You had to stand there near a bowl and half the time you
> couldn't get the stain out because they only allocated you so many
> rags. So you had to make them do. It was humiliating.

If sexual education was non-existent for child migrants in
Catholic orphanages, general education was little better. A Catholic girl recalled that, "You'd get one nun teaching three classes; it
was very basic. You were lucky to pass grade seven" (the most
basic elementary level). In the boys' orphanages, the length of
school depended on the weather. John McGillion is now unemployed and has little prospect of getting a decent job because of his
lack of qualifications.

> It sort of varied from day to day. If it was a real wet day, we'd spend
> the whole day in school, and then church. If it was fine, you went to
> school at nine in the morning and you were out by nine thirty, out
> working, building bricks, mixing concrete.

I do feel a little bit bitter about it. We should have really had more education, rather than be sort of manual labourers. Perhaps we could have had a better choice of skills then. To try to get a job nowadays, they want to know did you get any qualifications? A lot of those boys wouldn't have any, and that's how they would have missed out on a lot of jobs. I think myself that education was more important than to literally turn around and say, "Right, I'm going to teach you how to do this and teach you how to do that." Young blokes that left there, they could do a job; but to be able to put it down in pen and paper, I'm afraid that's what they lost.

There were often around ninety boys in the classes at Catholic orphanages. One boy reckoned that he had only had ten days' teaching in the whole time he was there. "My husband has had no education, he cannot read or write," said the wife of a Bindoon man. One boy who went to Clontarf was asked to leave by the school authorities at fifteen. They told him there was no point in his sitting exams, as he would never pass.

The education at the Fairbridge farm schools and the Barnardo Homes was better, children at least kept regular school hours. But a boy who went to Fairbridge Farm School in Molong in 1953, after having passed the eleven plus examination in England, said:

It was not exactly the environment in which any abilities could flourish. If I have a criticism to make, it's that I think a lot more effort could have been made with the brighter kids to help them to get somewhere near achieving their educational potential. There were never more than about a dozen from Fairbridge going to high school.

The boss [at Fairbridge] was delighted when I first went to Orange High School [the nearest high school] and won the language prize in the first year for French and Latin. He raised my pocket money from threepence to 1s. 3d. I don't think I was favoured, no. In many ways I think the brighter kids were disadvantaged because I don't think they were catered for. I mean, I succeeded despite the conditions. Children who came after me tended to start to do better, because I guess they could see someone who had actually done something.

This boy went on to teachers' college and ultimately became a doctor. He could have gone to university with a scholarship, but he didn't know it existed:

I had to say to the principal that I wanted to go on to the final years of school. No one came to me and said to me, you must go on. The attitude was not anti-educational, but kind of neutral.

George Wilkins, who was another of the few at Fairbridge who went on to high school, did poorly academically there because

Fairbridge did not provide him with a school uniform or school books and he felt an outsider.

> I will always remember at high school the headmaster standing at the top of the steps and saying, "Who is that boy without a uniform?" Fairbridge thought that no one else had a uniform, and why should I?
>
> If there were high school excursions, like sporting events, the whole school used to go and we had to have maybe 2d. for the bus and we had to go there and it was too far to walk. So I would go up to different school kids and say, "I need another ha'penny, I have a penny ha'penny," and sooner or later one would give me a ha'penny and ultimately I'd get a penny and go on until I got my 2d. I always got on that bus, but it wasn't easy. I couldn't go to school play nights: there was no transport. I always felt it.
>
> For lunch you would sometimes get one baked bean in a sandwich; or you'd have a mutton sandwich and the blow flies had attacked it and it would be full of maggots. But every day at recess I'd eat my lunch as I would be hungry and the rest of the day there was nothing. You had to wait till you got back.
>
> At the end of the fourth year, the principal at Fairbridge called me into the office and said I was to be apprenticed at Orange as a fitter and turner. I wanted to get far away from Fairbridge, but he said if I didn't do it, I owed them two years' farmwork [through being at high school]. I said, OK, I will do the farm work, but he said remember your sister is still going to be here and if you don't take this apprenticeship, it will be difficult for her. So that convinced me.

After tackling a wide range of jobs he decided, at the age of forty, to go to university and did very well. He subsequently went into business and did even better, becoming a millionaire. But he strongly feels that his success in later life had nothing to do with Fairbridge, except in the most negative of senses, "I think it was because of Fairbridge that I felt I had to do something to show that *despite* them I could win. But I have never felt they gave me anything."

Most children left the orphanages, schools and farm schools when they were fifteen as the schools could no longer claim money for their upkeep. Gordon Grant recalls:

> The night before I left, I was just told, "Tomorrow you are leaving." I did not know where I was going to work, what job I would get, where I was going to live. When I arrived at Bindoon I had a big suitcase and new clothes. When I left, I was without a penny in my pocket, in sandals, with no underclothes, just a pair of khaki shorts. They dropped me at the Catholic Child Welfare and said, "Those bastards will look after you."

He stayed at Bindoon until he was seventeen as the Christian Brothers told him that he would get two years off his five-year apprenticeship if he stayed to help them. But this wasn't true. "The employers did not want to pay you third year rates. And no family wanted to take on a kid from Bindoon. The only way we survived was working at weekends weeding people's gardens in order to pay for your board, because the Child Welfare department was three months behind in paying a week to the landlord."

The attitude to these youngsters by those employing them was one of master to slave. Another boy was also told abruptly that he was leaving Clontarf to go to work:

My first job was to go as a milk boy, but it didn't last very long. They spoilt their son and I was just a bit of shit, I was nobody. I went on the streets and got drunk. I hadn't learned to read or write. I worked in a hardware store for a bit and did a few robberies and ended up working with building companies.

These early child migrants in Australia had no hope of going straight into a professional job. Expectations for them all were low. The first verse of the Fairbridge School song went:

> We are Fairbridge folk, all as good as e'er
> English, Welsh and Scottish, we have come from
>   everywhere
> Boys to be farmers and girls for farmers' wives,
> We follow Fairbridge, the Founder.

But the boys went as farmhands, not farmers, and disappeared into the outback. One boy left Fairbridge Farm School at Pinjarra at fifteen and recalls going to work on a farm hundreds of miles inland:

I was put on a train and dumped at the station at 3 am. The farmer who collected me first picked up a mob of sheep. I was dog tired, desperate for a meal, and when we arrived he said, "This is your diggins" and pointed to a hessian bag hut. I crashed down inside, exhausted, and got a poke in the ribs and was asked what I was doing. "You'll have no sleep until you've fed the pigs and cows." It was nine at night before I got a meal. And I was too tired to eat at that time. It was pretty devastating. I washed in a bucket inside the hut and worked like a navvy for 12s. 6d. a week. Half of it was put into trust by Fairbridge and I never saw it.

Others in similar positions recall the heat, the relentless dawn-to-dusk working, the loneliness and the "stinking heat". Years after leaving the orphanage, having gone from farm to farm, one girl finally managed to become a nurse. She was spotted working in hospital by a nun who had been at her orphanage, who said, "Do you know, you're a credit to us, Marlene." "No, I'm a credit to myself," came the reply. All the child migrants emphasise how badly prepared they were for life outside the school – not even being taught how to catch a bus. George Wilkins remembers:

> I was totally without social graces and there was no one to tell you how to behave. Later in life I saw one of my reports which said, "Has ability but no punctiliousness." How do you learn punctiliousness? When I went to live in a boarding house, after I'd left school, there were about a dozen people living there and at night I would want to go to bed, but I was not capable of saying goodnight. I would always have to wait till everyone else had gone. I was exhausted, but I was not able to get up and say, "Goodnight, I'm going to bed."

For the girls it was often worse. Once they had reached fourteen or fifteen, they were sent out to be domestics on farms – "stations" – in the outback. Not only was the work backbreaking but, young and innocent and on their own without anyone to turn to, they were vulnerable to abuse. Two months after she turned fourteen, Sylvia Randall was sent to a farm "a long, long way from anywhere". "They didn't have any electricity and there was four children. I worked from seven o'clock in the morning till seven o'clock at night, for five shillings a week." After constant criticism from the farmer's wife, "they chucked me out" and she was returned to the orphanage and was immediately sent off again.

> I was sent to this farm, miles away. She was an ex-school teacher, she was rather nice actually. And he seemed all right, until he started to, you know, try doing things to me. Well, I didn't know what he wanted. I was laughing at something in the comics one day and he said to me. "Come out here." And I thought he was going to show me something outside and I still remember walking out of that door. And the next minute he grabbed me and kissed me. Nobody'd ever kissed me like that in my life. I felt really weird.
>
> Next morning he smiled at me and went off to work. And I said to her, "Your husband kissed me last night" not thinking I was hurting her. I didn't know a husband and wife had to be together. I thought if they kissed someone else it didn't worry nobody. But that night I heard her crying and I could hear them arguing about it.
>
> He got me in the shed once, and he was trying to touch me down below, and I knew that was rude. And I kept telling him that he was naughty, that he was not to do that. And then he started banging my head on the wall. He was really hurting me. I told him I wanted to leave and he said, "You're not going back." So I planned to run away

and somehow or other he found out I was gone and came and got me off the bus and back to his home. Then he rang up the Catholic Welfare and said, "We're sending Sylvia back. She's not happy here because I slapped her." And when I tried to tell them at the Orphanage what he'd been trying to do to me, they said that was impossible.

So I was sent to another farm. And I was bathing the little girl, giving her a good wash like you do with kiddies and she said to me, "Don't hurt me there, Sylvia." And I said, "No, I won't, love." And she said, "But it hurts." And I said, "Well why, love?" And she said, "Well, my Daddy touches me there." And, oh, I just had to get out of that place. So I went back to the Orphanage.

And I went to another place, and there was this missionary priest there, preaching hell and fire and all that. And he asked to see me in the church one day. And the people, they were Catholics, and they thought it would be all right. So I went. And this missionary priest, he had sex with me in the vestry. And I thought, well, what he'd done was wrong. So every time I went to confession, I'd confess this sin and ask if they'd forgive me.

Most of the children shipped off to Australia from Britain after 1945 were sent by the Catholics. The Fairbridge Society sent the next largest number, followed by Dr Barnardo's and, last, the Salvation Army. There was no official attempt made by the British government to assess the child migration scheme in Australia until 1956. Three years before that, John Moss made an unofficial, uncommissioned report for the Home Office, called "Child Migration to Australia." This only occurred because Moss told the Home Office that he and his wife were planning a visit so he was asked to look into child migration arrangements.

Moss visited all the institutions in Australia that received child migrants and all but one of those that had submitted applications for approval to take them. The one he missed was due to what he called his "deficiency in geography". He didn't know where it was and he didn't have time to go back and see it. This was how migrant children were protected. His report was short on substance. Eight paragraphs were devoted to "Ablution and Sanitary Arrangements" and his creative recommendation here was that special attention be given to providing more foot baths, and that hot and cold water should always be available for all types of such baths! The subject of pocket money merited four paragraphs, payments being considered "not altogether satisfactory".

There was no awareness in the report of how the children were being treated. Moss writes that he was "impressed by the thoroughness with which the interests of child migrants are safeguarded, and by the standards of care available". These superficial remarks were made at a time when children were already making official complaints about the extent of abuse – sometimes in the very institutes he had visited. Too many people who wrote reports on child migration frequently had a pleasant visit with the officials running the institution, and gullibly accepted what they were told. Moss concluded his report by saying:

> There seems to be a feeling in some quarters that it is wrong to send a child for whom a local authority is responsible some 10,000 or 12,000 miles away. If, however, members and officers of [the] Children's Committee had had the same opportunities as my wife and I of seeing the conditions under which the children are being cared for . . . I am sure they would have no hesitation in helping to fill the vacancies which now exist in approved establishments, and would adopt a general policy of sending a regular but small flow of suitable children . . . They would then not only be doing good to the children but helping in a small way to increase the English-born population of Australia.

As far back as 1875, Andrew Doyle had challenged the simple-minded view that the solution to the children's problems, and the colonies' emptiness, was to bring them together without a thought to the consequences. But John Moss airily accepted the idea that the children would be bound to settle down in their new country and was concerned only about the age at which they should be sent out – he believed five years should be the minimum age and twelve the maximum. With a report like this, it's no wonder child migrants saw themselves as unwanted and discarded. Moss even emphasised the total lack of thought for the children's own psychological welfare:

> There have been few cases in which parents have followed their children to Australia, but this is not encouraged as the child migration scheme is primarily for those children who have been deprived of a home life. They [selection officers] have been asked to do their utmost to select cases whose parents are not likely to follow them . . .

At the time this report was being written, in 1953, child migration was virtually ending in another country – New Zealand. Far more children had been sent to Australia than New Zealand after the Second World War but the New Zealand children on the whole suffered less abuse and disruption and were better protected, legally. Post-war families in Britain were actually encouraged to join the children and special arrangements were made for their supervision. They were all the direct responsibility of central government. Section 3 of the New Zealand Child Welfare Act, 1948, says:

> Every immigrant child shall immediately upon arrival in New Zealand be deemed to have been placed under the care and guardianship of the Superintendent of the Child Welfare Division of the Department of Education in all respects as if an order of committal in respect of the child had been made.

Although the Superintendent was legally responsible for finding a suitable home for each child, in practice he delegated this duty to suitable semi-official bodies. The end result was that instead of children being sent to a receiving Home on arrival, and waiting there until a family was found for them, a home for each was found before they arrived and they were collected by the adopting family as soon as the ship docked. Only when this did not work out would the child go to a receiving Home. As a further safeguard, Section 3 lays down the foster parents' duties – which were even stricter than those of a guardian. They were expected to maintain, feed, clothe and educate the child, see that he or she wasn't overworked and provide for its physical, mental and moral training. Furthermore, the home was to be regularly inspected by the superintendent to prevent any exploitation of the child.

Although New Zealand made a serious effort to oversee the children, the "regular inspection" often failed to materialise. One boy, whose family was later to join him, left for New Zealand in 1953, said, "No power, kerosene for lights, no heating or hot water for washing or bathing; light the copper, do your own washing; for a toilet, just the long drop. Ah, yes, I remember it well! And to top it off, not a sign of any welfare officer."

In 1956, a further, official, "Fact-finding report" on child migration from Britain to Australia was published. This time, more pertinent, precise questions were asked about the type of care given to these children. It formally covered the "reception and upbringing of migrant children by the various voluntary societies". The emphasis was on children living in communal Homes and institutions in Australia and its recommendations were clear. Migrant children should be boarded out with foster parents wherever possible. The practice of taking children from Britain, placing them in orphanages that were separate and isolated from Australian life in general, and family life in particular, should stop.

This recommendation attacked the very basis of organisations like the Fairbridge Society, or the Roman Catholic organisations, that placed children in farm schools or orphanages. Such institutions only allowed the children a minimal amount of mixing with the local community. The fact-finding mission stated that there should be adequate opportunity for children to be assimilated into Australian life, and made three recommendations:

1. Children should be encouraged to take part in the normal life of the community.
2. Arrangements for children to spend their school holidays in private homes should also be encouraged, preferably to the same foster home each time.
3. Children should be placed with these holiday foster parents if at all possible.

For once, the 1956 report did not come up with the usual tired clichés about children being a threat to society if they weren't removed from Britain or that they would be saved by the clean air and wide open spaces of Australia. Instead:

We heard often in the course of our discussion that widely-held view that many children whom life had treated badly would benefit by transfer to a new country where they could be given a fresh start, away from old scenes and unhappy associations. Few with whom we spoke seemed to realise that it was precisely such children, already rejected and insecure, who might often be ill-equipped to cope with the added strain of migration . . .
     We think that it will be agreed generally that the desirability of enabling children deprived of normal home life to be brought up in circumstances approaching as nearly as possible those of a child living in his own home applies with particular force to migrant children, who in addition to the basic need of children for the understanding and affection that lead to security, here experienced disturbance arising from their transfer to new and unfamiliar surroundings.

Fine words. Why weren't they carried out? The few humanitarian recommendations made in the history of child migration never became law. In this instance, the numbers of children being sent to Australia from Britain actually *increased* from 1956 to 1966, with boatloads of 750 to 1,000 children leaving. And still they were sent to communal institutions. Only after the mid 1960s did the whole scheme finally peter out. And there were practical explanations for this. Australia's economy no longer needed that type of child labour, while in Britain, the type of child sent overseas (illegitimate, abandoned, or where parents couldn't cope) was increasingly being placed in the care of their local authority.

The orphanages and farm schools the children were sent to in Australia were destructive environments because there was no basic foundation for emotional development. Many were scarred by the experience and found themselves unable to cope with adult relationships. Because records were deliberately withheld from them, they had no sense of identity or self-worth. The contempt which they experienced when, at fifteen, they were sent to work in menial jobs, often in farms hundreds of miles away, reinforced their feelings of worthlessness. No one questioned what was going on. No one seemed to recognise the ample opportunities for abuse. Reports were made to the government about the system and the organisation; but there were no reports about the children. Nobody asked the most important question: whose needs were being satisfied in all this?

10

The Children's Voices

The mass experiences of children – the manner of their exodus
from children's Homes or their own home, the journey, arrival,
what awaited them and their life from then until now – brings
home the enormity of the child migration movement. Memories
are still intense. The first wave of child migrants to Canada are in
their seventies, eighties and nineties but many are still in tears
when recalling their early life. Some in Australia have been so
traumatised by their experiences that they are only now, as others
have begun to come forward, able to speak openly about their
past.

Many of the agencies involved, told of these experiences, say
defensively that all *their* children had a lovely, happy time, that it
must have been other agencies, or that one or two lying and
discontented child migrants are stirring it all up. But too many
migrants have told of their harrowing, numbing experiences for
this to be true.

"You're going on a holiday"

Many of the children's Homes just packed off a bundle of children
overseas with no explanation. One girl remembers the Home
she was in "being emptied overnight" and that she would have
gone too had she not been ill. Some boys remember being told
of the attractions of Rhodesia at school; other children were
given a stark choice between Canada and Australia. Many remember their sad and bewildered parting with a parent or relation:

> When I was sent to Fairbridge, I was told I was only going for six
> weeks. My mother said, "You are going on a holiday for six weeks and
> you will be back." And I look back and think, that's what people are
> like, that's the real world.   *Seven year old*

> I remember coming home from school one day in England to find the
> furniture in the back yard and the house locked up. They had not paid
> the rent. I ended up in the Middlemore Homes. I never saw my mother

and father again, though I wrote to my mother. I was not asked if I wanted to go to Canada. There was no choice: you went in [to Middlemore] and stayed there until they had a bunch ready to go over. One year they sent a bunch to Australia and the next year to Canada. *Fourteen year old*

I was never told why I came [to Zimbabwe]. My mother organised it and presented it to my father as a *fait accompli*. I don't think my parents were very well off so they may have thought they did the right thing and were giving us a better life. At times I think it was very strange. How can you chuck your children out of the nest? My brother and sister and I were illegitimate. *Nine year old*

I was put in a home in Tunbridge Wells when I was very small and I was there for three or four years and they came round the school and said there was this opportunity to go to Rhodesia, Canada or Australia and when you are only six or seven, and Johnny Weismuller was the chap on the movies those days and you fancied yourself going to the jungle, this sounds exciting.

So they took you off for aptitude tests and the next thing I knew we were going up to London, and we went to the Charing Cross hospital to get injections for yellow fever and all those strange diseases, and that was the last time, by chance, I saw my eldest sister, who was about seventeen or eighteen and a nurse. There were all these little kids and she was handing out the injections and recognised my name. *Seven year old*

Those of us destined for Canada were one morning loaded on a bus and taken on a tour of London to see the sights – the Tower Bridge, Parliament Buildings, London Tower, Traitors' Gate, Big Ben and Madame Tussauds. We saw all this along with a lecture on our heritage with strong exhortations never to forget "Merrie Old England". Sometime toward the end of January we were taken to Liverpool by train and put aboard a ship named SS *Montclare*. We were kept aboard for two or three days before finally sailing. There were thirty-five boys in our group. We were located in the steerage and I will *never* forget the smell of paint and the close quarters.
Thirteen year old

My mother was not married and I had a brother. I don't think we were in straitened circumstances. We lived in a small village in Fife. I don't know how she came to get in touch with the Fairbridge scheme: I can't imagine any social worker running around our village, telling any grubby boys "OK to go to Rhodesia". My mother knew that unless she herself followed, that was the last she would see of me. I don't know what motivated her but she had been living in a tied farm cottage with my grandparents and when they died she lost her entitlement. If she made the decision to send me, she would have rationalised it in some way. I know my uncle was against it.

Eight year old

One evening I was called in by the then Mother Superior [of the children's Home]. She was a strict lady and I thought I was going to be in for some kind of telling off. "Have a seat, my child," she said. Then she started talking about being sent to Australia. Blimey, I thought, have I been that bad to be sent away? Mother Superior went on to say that I had been chosen, that it was a wonderful opportunity, not some kind of punishment. But that night in bed, I cried. I was so frightened of leaving the only home I'd ever had, of leaving my school friends, my only sisters, of leaving my best friend Pearl and never seeing any of them again. *Ten year old*

When I was about ten, three serious looking men visited the Home. The children were all lined up in the hall and asked, "Who wants to go to Australia?" "Me! me!" we all shouted, putting our hands up in the air. We thought it was an outing and we didn't go on many outings. A number of the girls were picked, I don't know why we were chosen, and we were told some more about the trip. The men made it sound like fun, there would be lovely fruit on the trees which you could pick out of the windows, and we'd get "aunties" and "uncles". We went for our medicals, had our tonsils out, and were put on a train to Southampton and then on to a boat. *Ten year old*

I lived with my uncle and he upset me one day and I went off into a sulk. And he came to me about a week later and said, "Do you want to go to Rhodesia?" And I said, "Too bloody true." He said, "At least if you organise a picnic there it isn't going to rain on you." I looked at my own son when he was nine and thought, how could I have decided at that age to go to another country? *Nine year old*

At two and a half my parents split up and I was put into care at Nazareth House in Cardiff. It was a condition of entrance into the Orphanage that a child was baptised a Catholic, so I was baptised under my mother's maiden name, presumably to reduce my father's chances of finding me. At the age of thirteen, I felt my luck had changed. The nuns at the Orphanage told me I was going to Australia. It sounded great, a land overflowing with milk and honey! My friend who was black was refused as Australia had an all-white policy. We had no idea where we were going, but we didn't care.

Thirteen year old

I was the one in our family who wanted to go. I was at Harmony Road Primary School in Glasgow and someone came around touting these black and white photos and said, "Who would like to go to Africa?" And I took my little pamphlet and trotted home and said, "I want to go." And my mother and father were separated and my mother did all sorts of jobs to make ends meet and feed us four kids. I was probably the most independent and over and above this was my health, I was asthmatic, and the doctor said, "You must get this child out of Glasgow." Bulawayo was called "the desert" because it's high and dry and hot. So Mother and we four children talked about it and the other three said, "If he goes, we go." And we went. I was ten, my brother seven, and my two sisters were six and twelve. *Ten year old*

One gentleman at the Home then asked me whether I would like to go to Australia, New Zealand or Canada. I wondered at the time why I felt so *funny* around the midriff. Now I realise that it was a loaded question and should not have been presented to a mere twelve year old in such a blunt manner. However, children in that day and age were not considered to be quite human, but rather some sort of creature to be whipped into shape as they matured.

I had to make a choice or, failing this, I suspect the choice would have been made for me, for it was quite obvious that I was going somewhere in spite of what I thought or did. I don't know exactly why I chose Canada as my future home, unless it was because I immediately thought of cowboys and Indians. Most English kids read about the wild west as seen through the eyes of Zane Grey and Deerfoot, the well-known Indian hero. *Twelve year old*

My parents had been judicially separated straight after my birth. I must have scared them off! I lived with my grandparents and we were as poor as church mice. But I was keen on scouting and had joined a scout group and through the person running it I got to know of the Fairbridge scheme and I asked what one had to do to apply. I was ten years old. I jumped at the chance and was most persistent. It was a great adventure – I was not too aware of the implications involved. I had never even ridden in a motor car! *Ten year old*

They notified him [my father] that I was leaving Middlemore Homes for Canada but he was in a pub and didn't come to say good-bye. *Nine year old*

The journey over

I can remember that we were on the boat and we had rice and I have never liked rice to this day. I had never been out of England before, I remember the sun was going down and it seemed so *lonely*. I remember crying. *Eight year old*

I just did not have any idea what was going on. I did not know what was happening. I was so bewildered. I was sick on the boat all the way over. *Nine year old*

The boat trip was a bewildering experience, as we couldn't relate to anyone. This woman looked after us and it's the first time we had seen a woman and not a nun – you don't see a nun as a woman. We were frightened and scared on the ship. It was an emotional journey. We were locked in our cabins, crying that we didn't want to go. And there were no answers.   *Eight year old*

You were going from one children's Home to another and when you were on the ship you were a bit apprehensive at going into the unknown, but at that age you did not understand, anything could happen. We were very fortunate as we were one of the few lots of children who actually went through the Suez Canal. We went through Zanzibar and it was very interesting. We could see the pyramids and elephants from the decks of the boat. There were about twelve of us in the party and we were accompanied by a house matron. We ran around the boat and we could have a hard time. If they caught us they would stick us under the salt hoses.   *Seven year old*

Before we left England, we were all given shorts and funny hats. We all hated these round hats and the night before we came out we shaped them into a man's hat, altering the brim, as they looked more like girls' hats!   *Eight year old*

I do remember one day. The captain of the ship had us all around with the hosepipes and we were bombarding the natives. I think there was some disease in the place, and that was our fun, we had to keep them off the ship.   *Ten year old*

On board I was sick all the time, I never saw the deck until we docked at Halifax. There were a lot of boys and girls came over. We hardly ever saw the boys, they were on one side of the ship and we were on the other. I was very scared. I never made any friends on the ship.   *Eleven year old*

The boat trip out was fantastic, we had classes in the morning and games in the afternoon. It was great fun.   *Eight year old*

When we came over we had luggage, caps, overcoats. No adult accompanied us. They put us on the boat in Liverpool in charge of the captain and we were aged from thirteen to fifteen and they thought we could take care of ourselves.   *Thirteen year old*

Arrival

It wasn't very pleasant. It was *frightening* really, a strange country. We came off the boat like we were sheep. When we got to the bottom of the gangplanks we were all separated, some of my friends went off in different directions and I didn't ever see them again. Then the group I was in, we were taken out to the bush to Bindoon; that was the most frightening part, right out in the bush. We thought it was the Black Hole of Calcutta.   *Twelve year old*

In Canada, they put us into Fairview Home, just outside Halifax. It was a big private Home. There was hardly any furniture at all, nothing fancy, just bare boards and some benches that we sat around on and no tables. We ate our meals in the woodshed.

We were there from the time we landed in Halifax until they found a place for us. I stayed there about three months. The younger ones were all taken away within two or three days. The reason was that up to fourteen, employers did not have to pay them wages. They were sent to school and worked for their board and of course they got them cheaper that way. The ones that were fourteen and over did not go to school and they had to pay us wages. I remember us sitting and crying after the others left, seven of us. We were very homesick.

Fourteen year old

I was very excited when I first saw land [Australia] and when we arrived there was a welcoming party. There was these funny furry looking fruits, peaches, it was very exciting and pretty. I didn't exactly like it all 'cause it was different, but I was very excited by it.

Eight year old

Before we left the ship they had a big do for us, gave us ice cream cones. And then we boarded the train to Belleville [Ontario, Canada]: it took five or six hours. We were put in the [distribution] Home then and taken up to our rooms and put in bed. I was frightened. I was sorry I had left and I cried and cried as I wanted to go back. I wanted to go to Canada, but when I got there I wanted to go back to Wales. I guess the other boys felt the same. We were wrestling around and the superintendent said that people would be going to choose us to work for them. *Twelve year old*

We landed in St John's, New Brunswick, and the first impression of the place was not too flattering. We were assembled at the gangway and marched off into the customs building, which closely resembled a huge barn. The outside of the building was in fact covered with pine lumber that I later came to know as barn board. The interior was no more comforting than the exterior, and if it was designed to make immigrants feel warm and comfortable about Canada, it failed miserably, at least as far as a group of young boys who weren't too happy about being there in the first place.

Clearing customs took about one hour, which seemed like an eternity to us. The furniture consisted of rows of low benches and two long wooden tables at which the customs people worked. The lighting consisted of single light bulbs suspended in two rows from the ceiling, which gave the whole atmosphere an eerie effect.

All in all our first impression of this wonderful land was not all that good. Little did we know we had not scratched the surface yet.

Twelve year old

The journey on the bus from Adelaide was unbearable. We opened the windows, only to be shouted at and told off by the nuns, who said, "Don't you dare open the windows and let the hot air in." But of course we didn't know better. *Nine year old*

I arrived in June. They must have thought Canada an awful cold place. I had a flannelette shirt on and a serge dress and a coat and two petticoats and a hat. I was met by a neighbour of the family I was going to, who took me up to Springfield, New Brunswick, where the people adopting me, they *called* it adoption, came to meet me. My brother went to a different home. *Eight year old*

We arrived in Fremantle, near Perth, and there were these nuns, just like the ones we'd left back in Hammersmith and I was expecting aunties and uncles. I asked where the aunties and uncles were, but no one replied. We were taken off the boat and sat down to our first meal in Australia, which was a large pink fruit. I hadn't a clue what it was and didn't want to eat it. I thought it was yucky, tasteless. But there was no choice about it, the nuns told us to eat it and you did. That water melon was my first taste of the promised fruits of Australia. We then went on a twelve hour bus journey to the orphanage.

Ten year old

We came out to Canada at a pretty good time, in May, but I was still homesick. I never knew home life at home, but I had never had such homesickness in my life. You did not know anybody and everybody made fun of you. I went down the store one time for a gallon of kerosene and he thought I was saying "calendar", except I had a gallon jug in my hand. *Fourteen year old*

We arrived at Fremantle and boarded this van at night and got to this enormous big place, with an enormous big dining room with aluminium cups and plates. We were stripped of our kilts and were strangers in a strange environment. *Eight year old*

The Australian kids were scared of us: they sort of stood back and looked at us as if we were freaks. And we found out later that the nuns had told them that they weren't allowed to laugh at us because we talked funny. We were lined up, about an hour after we arrived, and were told to take our chewing gum out of our mouths and drop it into this newspaper. And they put on a party for us, which was really a bit of a front, because the photographers were there and the newspapers. The reports of anything you read in the newspapers in those days was, oh, these girls have arrived and they're so happy. In actual fact we were made to write letters back to England, to the orphanages that we came from, once a month, to tell them how wonderful it was out here.

Day to day life

That first week we asked a terrible lot of questions. But no one would give us answers. We were asking, "Can we write to the nuns back at the Home?" And the nuns there said yes, but they were never ever posted. We found out afterwards that they wanted us to break contact with England altogether, wanted to keep us quiet. I did get one letter from a friend at the Home in England and I tried to write back to her, but they wouldn't give us any paper or anything to write on.

It was only this year a nun said to me that they were told with us English girls, "The first week, give them their freedom, let them do what they like; but the next week we will lay on the discipline." She made me promise never to mention her name.

I think they thought we were going to be dead poor, you know, with no good clothes. They were very disappointed that we didn't come in as waifs, beragged. The younger girls were told to be kind to us, "Because these children are not going to have any clothes". I think it was embarrassing for them to see that we were clothed. I had a beautiful tartan skirt, it was really lovely, and they gave it to one of the Australian girls. To this day I hate her.   *Ten year old*

I was sent off from the distribution Home at Sherbrooke [Province of Quebec] with a ticket to get off at a certain place in Ontario.

I was met at the station and was talking away and I thought stuck up people, won't even talk to me! And when the farmer was passing his place, he pointed to the land and to himself. It took me time to realise he was deaf and dumb; and so was his sister who lived with him. He had one hired man and a daughter and son. He was a great big hefty guy. I started to learn the [deaf and dumb] language and it was pretty hard, you were working most of the time. So one day he was trying to sign something and I did not understand it and he banged his fist down and his daughter said, "Dad says the only thing you learn is something to put into your mouth!" And that made me mad and I said I wouldn't learn any more. I did not like that first year: I would cry in the woodshed.

The first year here, the temperature was around forty to forty-five degrees below zero and in the sugar bush we made maple syrup and we had a pole outside and marked eleven foot of snow on it. I used to ride down the hill on a team of horses with the bells on. In winter they used to build up the fire. The water froze and the wind was dreadful.

I had been out here three or four months when my two big toes swelled up so bad and so painful, I had to split new shoes in order to wear them. I went to the doctor and he was going to cut my toes off but the deaf and dumb man said another man had had his toes off and had trouble ever since. It was so tender, when a cat ran over my foot under the table, I cried. I would sit down in the middle of the yard and massage my feet and cry with pain.   *Fourteen year old*

The nun would come in and she'd say, "Jesus, Mary and Joseph. Jesus,

Mary and Joseph." I'll never forget that and you all had to dive out of bed and kneel in the middle of the floor and say your morning prayers. And then you got dressed and then you went to church. And then from church you had your breakfast and there was prayers again! You had to say grace, grace before and grace after meals; and then before you went to school you had to say prayers again. And then at school you learned your catechism and you learned all about your religion, so there was religion again. I thought, my God, when I get out of the place I'll never go to church again! *Nine year old, Australia*

I worked there for nine years and was too frightened to say anything to anyone. No inspectors came round. The wife had a baby every year and a half and I had dirty nappies to cope with plus the housework and I cleaned out the stables and in the summer time I fetched hay and grain and also milked the cows.

My little church was about four miles away and in order to get away from the place, I used to walk to church on Sunday. I never went anywhere through the week, I worked *all* the time. She [farmer's wife] kept you in your place: she was strict.

People don't realise today what us kids went through: the meals and everything was terrible. I remember one Sunday night, it was porridge for supper – no treats of any kind and once a year we used to go to the seaside and got given a raisin bun. There were no hugs; maybe that is why I am a little bit that way.

Then this chap wrote to me when I was eighteen. He was one of the boys who was on the boat coming out and he said he had always looked at me and admired me and felt he would like to write to me and come to see me. And he was out west. And the farmer's wife said no, because maybe they thought something would come of it. And everything I did, they blocked it. *Eleven year old, Canada*

We used to have fun doing the polishing. The nuns didn't watch all the time, so we'd put the rag under the mop and one kid'd sit on the mop! We sort of arranged it because she had more weight to polish the floor. *Nine year old, Australia*

There was the farmer, his wife and some spinster relation there and no one else to help on the farm. The farm was a hundred acres and there were three horses, about six head of cattle, cows, pigs and chickens. I started work before the crack of dawn. In the morning we would get up anywhere around 4.30 am and we would go to the barn, milk the cows and separate the milk and then have breakfast, groom the horses, put them on a wagon and mow the hay or cut grain. Eleven o'clock would be our dinner time and then out to the fields again and then at 4 pm it was supper time. Then we worked on bringing the grain in and the old chap would stand in the barn door with the lantern and that was eleven at night. By the time the horses were in, you fell into bed.

I came out in May. They did clothe me but not the best. In the winter I wore heavy mittens and gum rubbers [top leather, bottom rubber], woollen pants, long johns [combinations], big flannel shirts, home-made socks. You had to wade through snow almost up to your waist.   *Twelve year old, Canada*

Nineteen days after we arrived at Fairbridge [in Bulawayo} it was Christmas and we hung up our stockings, and the next morning there was nothing in them because the seniors had come and robbed them while we were sleeping, and this was my first experience and you learned fast.   *Seven year old*

The farmer was a nice man but his wife was hard to work for, very nasty and hateful to me. She just seemed to go out of her way to make life *miserable* for me. It was all the little things. If you were cooking pancakes and you tore the pancakes when you turned them over, she would say, "If you don't stop tearing those pancakes, I will put your hand on the griddle." And she would say, "Don't put salt in the potatoes when you put them on, you put the salt in after you mash them." And I would forget and put the salt in and as soon as she found out, she got mad and said, "I will teach you to remember, you can go without salt for a week."

Sometimes I would go upstairs and I would sit and cry and I would pack my bag and think I am going to run away from here, and then I would sit down and think *where* am I going to run away to? I've got nowhere to go. And I would unpack my bag and go to bed and that was it. I did not know anybody, no one to go and tell. With no money, you can't do anything. And you haven't any friends and no way of making them because they would never let you out. They were always there with you, you were never with anyone alone to be able to tell them. They did not allow you to go out on your own, you stayed at the farm and worked and you went to church, the United Church, with them on Sunday and you never got the chance to talk to anyone. I used to get down on my knees every night and pray to God to get me out of there.   *Fourteen year old, Canada*

Breakfast was always porridge and bread and milk. We never had any morning or afternoon snacks. We had a plain lunch and tea. We never ever got supper. I used to be waiting for it, or something to fill us up, and it never came.

We didn't go to school half the time. On Monday and Thursday, I'd have to help all day in the laundry, washing, hanging it out and ironing, so I didn't get any school then. We used to work hard at the Orphanage. Even people that lived around there were surprised to find there was so many children there 'cause they never used to hear any noises. Saturday mornings, we'd work all morning, but the dormitories were the most highly polished floors you'd ever seen. You'd get six girls on the floor, polishing. And we'd work for people outside, for the government. We used to have to tie these real thick bundles of string up, for the abattoirs; and at one stage we were folding up a whole load of maps. No one even gave us a lolly for it.

I remember this nun used to bring out these lollies and if the Australians had money, she'd write it in this black book and they'd buy so many sweets. But did they ever give us a lolly? No way. It mightn't have been important to the others, but it was to me.

We'd often steal food and if we got caught, they'd say, "Well, why don't you ask for it if you're hungry?" So you would do the right thing, ask them for it, and they would say, "You greedy little things, get out of here." There'd be truckloads of oranges coming in, waste from farms most probably. But I can't remember ever eating one, ever having a glass of orange juice.   *Nine year old*

We had 6d a week as juniors for pocket money: 1d went to the Church and 1d went for the cinema. And when you went to high school, you got 1/- and we spend about 4d on cigarettes, sweets. Sometimes we would catch a train at night time, after lights out, jump on a guards van and go to Gwella, a hundred miles away [from Bulawayo] and do our thing there and catch a goods train back and be ready for school. Daytime we'd take our packed lunch, keep the brown bag, and fill it with sugar from the sugar refinery, there was piles of sugar, and then jump over the wall and go to town and sell it. Or we'd take biscuits. We used to steal all this to go to the movies.   *Seven year old*

It was my third day in Australia, I remember it very clearly because it was on my thirteenth birthday. I woke up and my upper lip was absolutely enormous. And Brother McGee – he was a good man – said, "You look dreadful. The matron says you've obviously got a rare mosquito bite and the best thing is for you to go to bed and stay there." Anyway, at night time, about half past seven, after their prayers, the boys were sent down into the hall. And there was a Brother who liked to see guys roughed up, in many ways, he made them all put on boxing gloves and beat the hell out of each other. Anyway, I was upstairs and the next thing, in walked this very grotty, dirty looking man, with a hard bald head and he'd been working out in the fields all day, but he was wearing a religious habit.

And he come in and sat on the bed and started talking to me and he said I had beautiful skin. And then he said in his room he had a special strap that he used for discipline on boys. And I thought, what's this got to do with me? And then he started asking about temptations. And I thought, oh God! And the next thing this guy has got his hands under the blankets, feeling my crotch area. Oh, I was scared! I was terrified! Thankfully this young lad who was a kid who hated boxing came into the room. And I was saved. He must have sexually molested *hundreds* of kids in the forty years that he was involved with orphan boys.

Thirteen year old, Australia

We used to have turns at milking the cows and feeding the chucks and the pigs. Christmas time was the best time of the lot. We always used to have a barbecue, a good old Aussie barbecue. There used to be a chap who came up every year and he'd dress himself up as Father

Arriving in Toronto. The Press remarked on their 'smart appearance and cheery spirit'.

(Barnardo Photographic Archive)

LINKS of EMPIRE welded by the Church

More Links Fresh from the Forge.

The Gibbs' Home, Sherbrooke, Quebec, and some of its old boys.

Canadian Links.

One of the many who answered the Motherland's call in time of War.

A Party of the Society's boys about to sail for Canada.

# of England Waifs and Strays Society.

P.T.O.

A fund-raising leaflet stressing the Empire links. 　　　　　*(The Children's Society)*

'An inspection – "Food all right?"' *(The Children's Society*

OFF TO CANADA.

(The Children's Society)

THE WORK IN AUSTRALI

A Party of Barnardo Boys and Girls just arrived at
Perth, W.A.

(The Children's So

En route to Australia, 1932.   (*BBC Hulton Picture Library*)

Rhodesia House, 1950: getting ready to leave.   (*Alan Price*)

Fairbridge boys'
group in what was
then Rhodesia.

'It built a hell of a
lot of independence in
people.'

Dormitories.

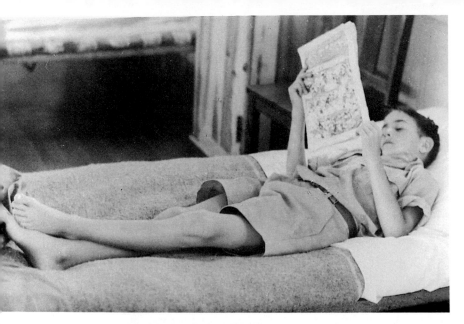

Fairbridge boy.

Royal inspection,
Fairbridge children,
Rhodesia.

Fairbridge girls.

Fund-raising advertisement for Bindoon orphanage, Australia.

Bindoon boys working the land.

above Building Bindoon from scratch
below part of the end result.

A Barnardo boy at Picton Farm, Australia.

A party leaves for Australia, 1950. (*The National Children's Home*.

Christmas. We'd all be waiting along the road, especially for Father Christmas to come. And the Irish Club used to come every year and they were fantastic. And we even had the West Perth Football Club one year and we played them football and beat them. But I think they might have let us! *Ten year old*

We had to fend for ourselves in the Farm School. Invariably you sorted out your own problems. Unless you are strong and adapt in later life there have been cases of Fairbridgeans doing silly things because of not being emotionally equipped. *Seven year old*

The Brothers used to actively encourage us to catch rabbits. And you'd be asked how many you caught. But there were occasions if you didn't catch enough you'd get belted, because if you had twelve traps, surely you must get at least eight rabbits, in your traps. And to make up the numbers, we would catch the odd cat in the trap. Because you would skin that cat, after you'd killed it, and of course cut the tail off, cut the ribs off, because cats' ribs are quite big and thin, whereas rabbits have got the saddle back. So you'd cut the ribs off and you'd throw the cats in with the rabbits. *Thirteen year old, Australia*

We used to have to wear knickers for a whole week and if we dirted them we got into trouble. I used to hate that. And we weren't allowed to run the water to wet our hair to set it, we got belted if we were caught doing that. So in the end we used to go into the toilet and pull the chain and use the flushing water. We weren't allowed to wear low-necked dresses to a dance and we were never allowed to mention a boy's name. That was my sex education. *Nine year old, Australia*

I was expected to be up by 6.30 am to do chores and then have breakfast and then I went to school, although school was over in June. And then I would go home and usually do more chores and mow the garden, and more chores, always chores. And no light or electricity. I liked to read, but you couldn't read once it got dark. It was pretty dull, just bed and up the next day. Then in June it was hay and crops and taking off the harvest. There was no one to play with: you just did *chores*. It seemed that my whole life revolved around these chores. There were chores in the morning and chores at night, chores on Sunday and every other time that I thought might be a free time to do something else. I didn't have to count sheep in order to go to sleep, I just counted chores. The farmer and his wife were very reticent and did not talk a lot: just sat and read the paper. There were no books. I don't think they knew when my birthday was: I don't think I even remembered my own birthday after I got off the boat.

On top of all this I was very homesick and lonely. I would say that for the first two or three years, all I could think of was getting back to England to a normal way of living. We hardly ever left the farm and there were not a lot of visitors. I suppose I did not work too well or too willingly because things deteriorated to such a point that, by fall, they had decided that I would never make a farmer and I had better be sent back to Toronto.   *Thirteen year old, Canada*

I was on the top of his huge statue once, just finishing the column; they were hard granite rock. And another boy and myself had actually finished completing it. And then this Brother came through the bush, shouting and swearing and telling us to get down here, get down. And we knew we were in for a hiding. I don't know why but that was just his nature. And we got down and he started belting us round the head and the body with this big stick. Well, this other boy had more common sense and courage than what I had, he went running off in the bush. And I never saw him again in my life.

Thirteen year old, Australia

I went back to ask the farmer's wife for my money coming to me and she said, "You haven't got any money coming to you" and she had it all wrote down on a piece of paper: lamp chimney had got broken, and they would crack when you went from a hot room to a cold room. She even had a cord of wood broke down because I left the store open. So that it all came to the money she owed me and I did not get it. It was supposed to be $36 she owed me, $8 a week.

I did not even bother to write and tell the Home as I did not think it would do any good. She had not bought me clothes the way she should have. The first winter I was there I wore my summer coat and straw hat until the end of January. I had to wait for the January sales before she bought me a winter coat and hat. I remember wearing that straw hat in an open sleigh for nine miles. I remember that trip so well as I had to stable the horse at the hotel and the man who was helping her said, "Who is that you have standing there?" And she said, "That's just the girl from the Home." And he said, "They're pretty poor trash, ain't they?" And she said, "Yes, they are."   *Fourteen year old, Canada*

Leaving the institution

Children sent out to orphanages and farm schools found themselves pushed out to work on farms or in some menial occupation, when they were sometimes only thirteen or fourteen. There was little chance of them ever following a career of any sort, let alone one that they would like. They went from a life of isolation and hardship to precisely the same life elsewhere.

They didn't have any electricity and there was four children. I worked from seven o'clock in the morning till seven o'clock at night, for five shillings a week.

One Sunday I come home from church and she had every dish out of the cupboard, for me to wash up again. And every one had yolk on it – you know, I couldn't see the yolk with the lamplight at night, because they used to take the great big lamp into the lounge to read the daily papers and I'd have this tiny little thing to wash up with.

Nine year old, Australia

I was sent out to a farm when I turned fifteen and I hated it. There was not another house for miles. I was cut off from all the girls in the orphanage, from the only friends I ever had, cut off again. You know, you sort of got the feeling that wherever you were going to go, through your life, you were going to be sent away somewhere. *Eight year old*

When you were about to leave, they gave us all this front bit of assessing you to see what you would be good at. And I showed pretty good signs of being a good dressmaker. In actual fact my grandmother was a very good dressmaker. And they said to me, "Oh, you're leaving next week." And I said, "Oh yeah, where am I going?" "Oh, you'll see."

Next week I was taken to Calvary Hospital: I didn't even know it was the hospital when I got there, because I was taken round the back way. I was shown to the nurses' quarters, where they all had little rooms. It was so small. I thought, "Oh, I thought I was getting away from this sort of thing." The next morning I was told to report to a particular nun, who gave me a white uniform and a little veil to wear. And I said to her, "Where am I?" And she said, "We're at Calvary Hospital, didn't you know?" And I said, "No. I thought I was going to be a dressmaker." And she said, "No, you're going to be working in the X-ray department." You just didn't argue.

We were told, when we left the orphanage that we were to report to the Father at the Catholic Welfare. And this is where it all fell apart, because nobody cared about us once we left the orphanage. Nobody came up to check to see if we were all right. *Eleven year old, Australia*

There was no say about leaving the Orphanage. I was packed on a bus with a name tag on me and sent to work on a farm in a place called Moora, a small and desolate place. I was met by an old bloke who took me up to the farm. It seemed a big place to me: it was about a mile from the farm entrance to the house itself. Once we got there I was shown where I was to live. It was a cubbyhole next to the pantry, about two foot six by five foot.

After that, it was up each morning at six and then cleaning, looking after the babies – there were four of them – and cooking for the shearers and farm hands. I was terrified of them, especially the Abos.

After two years, I packed my bags and holding my two small suitcases, ran away, vaguely marching down the long rural roads. I was picked up by the welfare officer who had been called out by the farmer, and returned to the farm. Refusing to stay, I was packed back to the nuns. *Ten year old, Australia*

I used to come top in every subject and wanted to go on to college. But the places went to two Australian girls who did far worse than me in class. I was sent to a farm 300 or 400 miles away.

I was just the maid. They had six kids and the eldest bossed me around like anything and if I said anything back his father would get out the rolling pin and hit me 'cause I was being cheeky. I don't know, maybe I was cheeky, but I thought to myself, this is not for me, I am fifteen, I want something better out of life. So after a few months, what I did was I packed my gear during the night and I sneaked my way out towards the paddock and I saw this trailer go by and I waved it down and I said, my mother's sick in Adelaide, please drive me back. And he did. When I got back I went to the Orphanage and refused to go back. They were angry but they sent me to a hostel and I worked in a chocolate factory. *Ten year old*

The farm I was sent at thirteen was in the middle of blooming nowhere. It was slavery. I used to start at five o'clock and finish late at night, all for 7s. 6d. a week. They didn't have electricity, it was all kerosene lamps and wood stoves. I had to do housework and dairy work and cooking because she couldn't do anything, she had polio. So I used to do the washing and they had an old hand-washing machine. That bloody old thing, you sat there and it was like a big tub, you know, and it had a handle on it. You used to have to boil everything in the copper first, because there was no electrics. And it was that bloody heavy, because I was only a kid, you know. *Ten year old, Canada*

If I'd have stayed in England, I would have been allowed to finish secondary school; I could have gone to teacher training college and I could have coped with it easily. I don't find study difficult.

Everyone of us, when we left school, was put into domestic service. You see, we had nowhere to go. We needed live-in jobs. I went to the Dominicans to be a nun. I'd expressed a wish to join, but I was hoping I could be a teacher first. I would have liked a bit more time, but they put it over me that I had to join at sixteen. I thought, well, if I could learn to be a teacher in the Order, it wouldn't be so bad.

But they wanted me to do the lay sister work, which was the cooking, the cleaning. So I had years and years of more hard labour. Up at five o'clock in the morning, lifting great big kerosene tins of coke. I got to the stage I was just so physically and mentally run down, I didn't know who I was.

I wanted to do teaching and I did do two years' practice teaching. But because I liked it, I wasn't allowed to do more. That was their idea: if you liked something, you were deprived of it. You had to be *humiliated*, you had to be *humbled*. *Eight year old, Australia*

11

"I'm an orphan. Please help me find my mother"

John McGillion was fifty before he found out that he had a twin sister. Both had been placed in the same Catholic Home in Northern Ireland when they were toddlers, and then segregated. His sister, Tilly, had remained there but when John was ten he was sent off to Australia.

He had a vague feeling that there was someone. "I could just sort of picture that I did see a little girl," he said. "I used to often wonder whether I had a family and it was only when I was older, in my forties and getting on to fifty, that I thought, *who* am I? *What* am I?" He had tried before, unsuccessfully, to discover something about himself. "It was embarrassing to me, not having a birth certificate. I'd be asked a lot of questions: 'Do you have any relatives? Who's your next of kin?' And I used to say, 'I don't know. I'm afraid I don't know.' Some of them used to say, 'What do you mean, you don't know?' I says, 'I never knew my relatives.' I even had to get an affidavit to join the army."

John's search first began about 1958. For years, on and off, he wrote letters but "I got no answers from anyone. No one explained nothing to me. I wasn't very happy. I mean, if they'd only had the decency and courtesy to write back and say, well, we tried to locate your birth certificate."

He finally tried writing to Dublin and – thirty years after the search began – his birth certificate was sent to him and for the first time he discovered his full name and where he was born. He wrote more letters and then he received a reply from the secretary of the school he went to in Ireland, it said, "We have reason to believe, through our records, that you had a twin sister."

"It was the first time I knew definitely that I had a twin," said John. "I cried for nearly a week after reading that. But surely to goodness someone could have at least told us that we had relatives? Someone did know. Someone *must* have known. Was it too much trouble to let us know, or didn't they want us to know?"

John's twin was finally traced, living in a small village in Omagh, County Tyrone. "I spoke to her for the first time. It was incredible, after fifty years, to be able to speak to your own flesh and blood. It was like winning the biggest lottery in the world. Then I started writing that many letters to her, I was getting cramps. So I decided, well why not make a tape. I sang some of the Australian songs and I explained to her about Aborigines and all about Australia here. It fascinated her."

When he flew over to Ireland to meet his twin, he said he found it almost impossible "to say what is in my heart".

To be able to step off a plane, especially in the land where you were born, and to really know nothing about it. Everything was so strange to me. It was like my life starting all over again but in reverse! It was a frightening experience – not knowing what to expect. I said, well, the first thing I will do, rain, snow or hail, is to go on my hands and knees and kiss the ground. And I did. I felt like hugging the ground. The particular spot I managed to pick was a big pool of water, but I couldn't have cared less!

I really honestly never thought I would ever see the family again. But as my twin sister said to me when we had a private talk, she said, "I always knew in my heart." And I said, "Well, Tilly, I have always had that feeling. And as I grew older and older, that feeling became stronger and stronger."

I've always been very tense and now at last I feel contented, *happy*. I can just let my head go free.

Child migrants like John, ruthlessly denied any information about their background, have no roots and no identity. Those of us who take a family for granted know nothing of the desperation of the child migrants to discover whether or not they have a single living relative. When you talk to them, many break down in tears, desolate.

Pamela Smedley was sent out to Australia when she was twelve but she has never taken out Australian citizenship and is obsessed by her need to find out if she has a family, "an uncle, an aunt, anyone would do".

I've never had a sense of belonging to anybody. Just being able to say "my mother", "my father" or "my sister" once, would be terrific. It would give me some identity. Because you feel as if you've got none – you're nobody, you're nothing. No roots at all. People in Australia say, "Where are you from?" "England." "Oh, you came out with your parents?" "No." A lot of people don't understand that you could be sent out alone. I even introduce my girlfriends, the ones that came out from England, as my sisters, just as a joke. But it's not that kind of blood relationship, I suppose. I've never had a feeling of security or safeness and I really think, deep down, that's the cause of the vacuum I feel. I've got a family and I've got children, but that doesn't fill it.

Pamela's lifelong feelings of desolation are echoed by Denise Trowsdale, who was sent to the same orphanage as Pamela.

I feel so alone, not lonely, *alone*. I want someone to accept me as I am. That's the thing I find hard. People don't accept me as I am, I don't know why. But a parent would, you know. I feel I'm on this earth all on my own. It's crazy, isn't it? It's like being out in a wilderness. It's a feeling I can't forget all my life. I have always wanted to have someone that belonged to me. No identity, I suppose they call it.

Christmas is hard. Christmas and Easter and the times when families get together, that's when I feel it. I'd love to have a mum to give a present to, to buy her something nice and have her spoiling my son. You see, he has no grandparents. My husband's parents are dead.

Other child migrants were equally emotional:

I would like to know about my mother even if it's not possible to see her. I'd like to know what it's been like for her because no mother can forget a child of her womb. I'm sure I have a relative somewhere in the world.

I have two children of my own, who of course have an identity and know who they are. I am forty-five years of age and still have no identity.

I know it sounds as if I'm living in the past, but I'm not living in the past. I want some form of identity, I want to know where I come from. This has been on my mind for *so* many years.

One woman, who had managed to trace her relations, felt quite different afterwards. "People in Australia have never known me more confident in myself," she said. "And it's *beaut* to be able to say, 'My sister in England, my brother in England'. I can talk about England with belonging. When I got there, I just cried. This could have been my home, my country!"

Age only increases the longing to find family. Child migrants in Canada, now mostly in their seventies and eighties, still have a deep need to find any remaining relatives in Britain. It's a need that is passed on to their children, who know hardly anything about their parent ("My mother told me her life was too painful to talk about") and who may worry about their genetic background and want to trace the lost half of their family.

Charles Devonport, now in his mid seventies (see Chapter 2), was obsessed for over forty years by what he called "Project: Find

Mother" (being illegitimate, he never knew his father). Unlike so many of the child migrants who were told they were orphans, he at least knew his mother was alive when he left Nottingham. His last memory of her was at the railway station, when, as part of a group of children, he was leaving England.

> I always thought to myself, some day I'll go back and find her; but I never had any money. Eventually, as I got older, the resolve to find my mother became stronger. But I didn't know how to go about it. When I joined the army, immediately the thought came into my head: when I go to England I'll go to my mother's house and I'll say, "I'm home, Mother, I'm back!"

He became preoccupied about meeting her:

> If I find her living, now what will I say? Suppose she's old and ill and her mental faculties are not that good? Maybe she, after all these years, will have genuinely forgotten about me. What'll I say? I can't just barge in and say, "Hey, Mother, I'm your son, I've come back!" She might say, "I don't have any son." You know, I had it all planned out. My wife and I were going to approach it gradually and slowly, get the minister, or somebody she knew, to introduce us. I was thinking of all ways to get there without shocking her or hurting her.

At first he found a neighbour who thought that his mother had died a year after he left for Canada. But he went on looking for information about her. It was a long, unrewarding business, writing letters to anyone he thought might help, including newspapers. "She was my mother. And that to me was enough to carry on the search. I just wanted to find her and tell her that I loved her." In the early 1960s he became better off financially and made a redoubled effort to trace her.

> If she was dead, I'd find the grave, and if she was living, I'd get in touch with her. I got a book on genealogy and hired several people but they all turned out to be nothing but con-men. In the end I did get a good woman and decided to pour money into the project and keep on going.
>
> I was thinking I'd never find her because there's so many people, so many millions of people, in England, and there were so many Nellie Devonports, we found *twelve* Nellie Devonports – that's my mother's maiden name. Several of them were born the same year as my mother – 1888.

The genealogist Charles employed finally traced his mother, to find that she had indeed died – but only six years previously:

> I just went outside and let the tears flow. I was still hoping that we'd find her alive, although I knew she'd be very old. I got in touch with a

gentleman who makes tombstones and I got one placed on the grave and made arrangements for a memorial service.

Standing at his mother's graveside, he spoke tearfully to her:

I was thinking, you know Mother, that I wish I'd found you while you were living. We could have exchanged views. I could have told you what I've been doing and we could have got to know each other and you could have told me who I am – that's important to me, to know who *I* am.

The way reunions with a parent were deliberately prevented by the withholding of records has traumatised and embittered many other child migrants. John Brookman, who was sent out to Australia from the Middlemore Homes in Birmingham in 1939 to Northcote Farm in Australia, which was in association with the Fairbridge Farm Schools, and then to Fairbridge in Molong, was equally devastated when he, too, found he had missed being reunited with his mother because her address was withheld from him. "I was sent out here knowing absolutely nothing about my relations," he says. "I was determined to find out if I had a mother and father and perhaps a sister. But Fairbridge told me nothing. They virtually said, 'there's nothing in the record book'." The reason for this only became clear years later, when he finally got his file and found a copy of a letter, dated 18 November 1943, from the Fairbridge Farm School headquarters in London, to Middlemore Homes, saying:

Thank you for your letter of 11 November with birth and baptismal certificate in respect of Michael [John] Brookman. We shall keep his birth certificate on file here (as the boy is illegitimate) but we will, when writing to Northcote about the "unknown sister", send the baptismal certificate.

Unaware of this, John tried to locate his parents through various sources like the Red Cross and the Salvation Army but to no avail. In 1983 when he was fifty-three, he wrote to Fairbridge and finally received his full birth certificate, which he found contained more details about his parents and his mother's address. He gave this to a genealogical society and asked them to search for her. They found out about her within six months and told him she had died four years previously. He could easily have traced her at the address on the certificate when she was still alive and he cannot talk about it without tears:

I can understand, I suppose, that back in 1943 when I was twelve, they might not want to give you this information. But they had no right to keep a legal document from you after you were twenty-one. She was alive and well when I was twenty-one, running a boarding house in Eastbourne, and she owned her home. I could have gone to see her. What the hell was Fairbridge playing at? I feel savage about it.

Once in touch with the rest of his family, a cousin – who had previously not known of John's existence – asked the Fairbridge Society in London for further information. In 1985 John received a letter from them saying, "We have now received a copy of your file from Liverpool [where the records of Fairbridge children are kept] and enclose copies of its contents . . . As you will see, many efforts were made in the past to find your mother but to no avail."

John's mother left her money to others but though members of his family benefited, John was not mentioned in the will. This is what can happen when organisations play God with children's lives.

Not all child migrants are bitter however. One man who had been sent out to Fairbridge Farm School in Pinjarra, Western Australia, firmly signed his letter "Australian citizen", and wrote:

I believe the "transportation" gave me a chance to be part of a newly developing nation, to develop a new identity. I went from being an abandoned child to being an Australian citizen in a land being developed by "new" citizens.

I will [soon] arrive in England to meet my mother and sister and family after nearly forty years. Although I am doing this to discover my roots, I am more concerned in being able to show my mother that the pain of those missed years was somehow worth it.

"The pain of those missed years" has been made worse for the majority of child migrants because they grew up in the false belief that they were orphans. This was not true: hardly any were. Sometimes children were just told, "You have no family, there is no one back home." Some were specifically told that their parents were dead, that they were killed in car accidents, that they died in the war. This was conveyed so convincingly that the children stopped asking constant questions: where is my mother? Where is my father? Why am I here? Do they know I'm here? Can I write home? Why can't they be found? Did you ask them if I could come here? One woman said: "Kids in those days had no rights. When I was in Barnardo's I asked about my father. They lied to me. They told me he was a good man who had gone off to war and got killed." He was actually still alive and the owner of an estate in England.

There is understandable anger and unhappiness at the way records have been deliberately suppressed.

Recently we went for a holiday overseas and I had to have a passport. When I went into the Post Office, the man in there quite rudely said to me, "Don't you even know your mother's name?" And imagine how that *hurt* me. Anyway, I thought I had to do something. So I rang the Community Welfare Services and they looked into the files and found a birth certificate with my mother's Irish address on it. All these years it had been sitting in the files in Perth.

And within a month I received a letter back from an uncle. It shocked the family when I wrote and said I'd been migrated to Australia at the age of four. They thought I was adopted in Ireland. I found out my mother had only died four years ago. It's just such an emotional thing. I was angry at the migration people here, and at the orphanage, for not giving me that birth certificate when it was here all the time. It was devastating to have missed her by just four years. I could have got to know her twenty-five years ago.

My friend, who was in the same orphanage as me, wanted to go to England four years ago and went to immigration to get a British passport and she found she did not even *exist*. How do you feel when someone turns around and says, "There is nothing here, you are no one." She's forty-eight now, she would have been about seven when she came out here and they told her there are no records, she doesn't exist! Yet how many farms did she work on. How can there not be records? Why has it all been hidden?

It makes tracing families difficult, if not impossible. Birth dates were treated in the same cavalier fashion. One boy who had been at the orphanage at Bindoon for over a year, asked a Christian Brother there why he had never had a birthday like some of the other boys. "Well, today's Our Lady's Day," he was told, "so you may as well make it today."

The child migrants' increasingly desperate and failed attempts to find out information about themselves and their families led to the remarkable story of the setting up of the Child Migrants Trust.

In 1986, an Australian woman wrote despairingly to The Triangle, a post-adoption group in Nottingham. Set up by a social worker, Margaret Humphreys, it is a unique group which helps those who have been adopted as well as natural parents and adoptive parents. The letter said:

I left England as a very small child on a boat to Australia with other children and I've no idea who I am. I've never been adopted, never been fostered, please can you help me as I originate from Nottingham.

Margaret Humphreys wrote back to Australia explaining that she only offered a service to people affected by adoption. The reply came back: "Why not? Why can't you help me?" The underlying message was, "As I've not had the privilege of a family life, I suppose I don't deserve your help."

By coincidence, a member of the Triangle group had managed to find her brother in Australia some years before. He had been in the care of East Sussex County Council and when she first contacted the Council it said it had no record of him, apart from the fact that he was in their care and the Secretary of State gave consent for him to go to Australia. Looking at these two accounts, Margaret Humphreys was faced with a piece of social history which she knew nothing about – the emigration of children from children's Homes operated by charitable voluntary agencies and, to a much lesser extent, from Homes run by statutory bodies. Her colleagues were equally incredulous at the idea of a large-scale movement of children out of Britain after the Second World War.

Margaret Humphreys ordered a copy of the Australian woman's birth certificate. It was the first of hundreds of such difficult searches. What were the circumstances in which a child could be left in a children's Home and shipped off, when only tiny, to Australia? And why Australia? And what for? What were they going to do when they got there? In this case, the agency concerned could tell her nothing to help her find the mother, all they had was a sad letter from her. It took further painstaking research to trace her. When Margaret Humphreys knocked on her door forty years after she had given up her child, within a minute she said she knew why Margaret was there.

> She told me she thought that her daughter had been placed for adoption and was living with a family in England and she naturally had no idea that she'd been sent to Australia.

To try and find out if there were others who wanted to find their families, Margaret Humphreys put a two-line advertisement in a Sydney newspaper. After consulting with the British Association of Social Workers, she travelled to Australia in conjunction with the *Observer* newspaper in 1987, to see those who replied. What she found shocked her:

> I went out to Australia to interview people who wanted to know about their roots, who wanted to find out if they had any family. And I was confronted with their childhood experiences, which were absolutely appalling. I was left feeling horrified and found it quite unbelievable that hardly anyone had heard of the plight of these people.

In order to offer a service to any child migrants needing help, Margaret Humphreys established the Child Migrants Trust on her return. She was seconded to the Trust for three years, from

December 1987, by Nottinghamshire Social Services Department.

Over 1,000 child migrants wrote to the Trust for help within the first year. The need for help remains overwhelming. If children do not understand why they have been removed from their natural parents, if they are starved of love, treated with contempt, cruelty or as if they had no feelings, then the emotional damage they suffer lasts into adulthood. The hundreds of letters the Trust receive express bewilderment and a deep sense of rejection by family and country. Today the child migrants feel they are the forgotten people. When Margaret Humphreys established the Trust, "People said, well, there may be thousands over there, but why do they want to know about their parents? It's just a few malcontents you've seen. But then the letters started to pour in: very sad letters, very desperate letters." Some were ten or twenty pages. They emphasised the senders' lack of identity, lack of confidence and confusion about their status.

I am an orphan, could you please help me find my mother.

I don't really know where to start, I'm so nervous. I don't have a birth certificate. I don't have anything. I sincerely hope somebody can help me.

I'm shaking, shaking as I write this letter. This is the first time I've allowed myself to think about some of these things again.

Unknown to some children, their names were changed. Sometimes they were copied down wrongly. Sometimes children with one Catholic parent and one non-Catholic were baptised and renamed when they were placed in a Catholic Home. Pamela Smedley saw her birth certificate for the first time in 1988. When she did, she found out that her first name is in fact Elizabeth. And Maureen Briggs describes the shock she had when she first left her Australian orphanage and went to work. "I clearly remember being made to sign a wage book." This contained an extra surname. "I said, 'Whose name is that? I don't know that name.' They said, 'Don't you know your own name? That's what we got from the nuns. Fancy not knowing who you are.' I felt a fool, an idiot. I didn't even know my proper name. I just went to my mattress and cried all night."

Another woman said:

When I went nursing, I had to have a birth certificate and I wrote to Somerset House for it. That's when I found out that my real surname was different. I had to get married under that name later and not the name by which I was known.

The Trust not only has to work with information that is scant or incorrect, but has the further problem of interpreting it. For instance, if the birth certificate says the parents were married, *were* they married? Or did the mother just register the child in the father's name and claim that they were married? What if there was no marriage? Did the mother marry someone else? In the circumstances, it is a long and laborious job to trace a person's movements some thirty or forty years ago. Many give up trying to research their family on their own and write to the Trust asking for help. One of these was Dorothy Chernikov who went to the Goodwood Catholic orphanage.

> I'm so angry with the agency that sent me out. I've written to them from the age of twenty and got no satisfactory reply, ever. They have just swept me under the carpet. And that hurts. I mean, they haven't told me anything. If I ever get to England, I would go to them and say, "Look what you've done to me."
>
> I am enclosing letters I have sent and received without much luck. I am hoping and praying you can give me other information and places to write to about finding my mother or any family. It's so disappointing to get letters back here in Australia saying that they have no record of me in England. I would be delighted and really appreciate it if you could get in touch with them as I feel these people have a lot to answer for. You see, this is where my mother went for help in the first place when I was born, and they are not answering my letters.

Dorothy enclosed the last letter she had received. The irritated reply to her letter was:

> I am writing to you again in response to your background.
>
> I feel there is very little I can add to the previous correspondence. It appears that children from England were evacuated to Australia under the Commonwealth of Australia Government Emigration Scheme.

It was particularly important to Dorothy to find her family because she had had her engagement broken off after her father-in-law to be had quizzed her at dinner about her family background. She explained to him that she was brought over to Australia from an orphanage in England and didn't know her parents. "You don't even know where you came from?" he shouted, and she heard him talking in the kitchen to her fiancé, saying, "Look, she doesn't know her folks. If you marry her I'll disinherit you." She said she felt like an outcast: "And yet we're not ratbags, far from ratbags."

She had been given heavy medication and every time she got upset at not hearing from the agency, she would "pop a pill, to forget. It wasn't that I was a drug addict, I just did it to fall asleep for a few hours and forget it." A psychologist eventually told the psychiatrist treating her, "Dorothy does not need any medication. *Talk* to her."

The Trust made enquiries into her family for her. Despite the repeated letters she had received, telling her that no information was available, the Trust found her family. It took time because Dorothy had been given incorrect information about her mother.

Almost all those who contact the Trust have similar stories about the lack of help from the agency or organisation that sent them overseas. One man, Harold Jones, told the Trust he had originally been placed in a Catholic orphanage when he was one, then sent to Western Australia in 1954, when he was nine. He ended up at Clontarf Orphanage where, like so many other children there, he was sexually abused. His younger brother was also sent out. He told the Trust that when he had written to the Birmingham Diocesan Rescue Society, who sent him out, asking why, he was told:

> Concerning the reasons for sending you to Australia, I cannot find any specific reason as far as you are concerned. I know that at the time Australia was looking for people to go and live there, particularly young people who would grow up in the country and benefit from it, both materially and culturally. A large number of children who had little or no ties in this country went out there and did very well, just as the children before them went out to Canada. All I can say is, at the time it was obviously felt that you would benefit from emigrating.

He was also told that his father had left his mother shortly after he was placed and that the last note on his file showed that his mother had gone to the office in Birmingham in 1960, to say she was going to London. She gave no forwarding address. The letter ended: "All this happened a long time ago and the possibility of tracing your parents would be remote."

This has proved true. Although Harold returned to Britain when he was twenty-seven, he has been unable to trace his family and is no longer in touch with his brother. He is under psychiatric care, although he says this is not necessarily due to his childhood experiences. After receiving the letter from the Rescue Society, he realised that he had not been singled out for special punishment, but his conversation still returns constantly to what preoccupies him: his mother and his inability to find her, or other members of his family.

The reason many child migrants believe that they were singled out for punishment is that, like Harold, they cannot understand *why* they were shipped off from Britain. It was, in fact, common practice for children's societies to insist that the natural parents sign "offers of acceptance" which usually contained an emigration clause, giving the society the right to send the child to one of the Commonwealth countries involved with child migration. The clause was often invoked. Edward Lewis was placed by his mother in an orphanage run by the Fairbridge Society at the age of six. When his grandfather heard of this, he declared that no child in his family ever went into an orphanage and tried to get him back. But the Fairbridge Society said the child had already been legally signed over to them and, furthermore, he was already on his way to Australia with no possibility of being returned.

When Edward was sixteen, his grandparents wrote to the Fairbridge Society to make arrangements for his return to Britain. The Society replied saying they had placed Edward on one of their farms. In fact, because Edward was sixteen, he had the choice of writing home but he says that he wasn't told of his grandparents' enquiries. When he was eighteen, his grandparents wrote to Fairbridge Society again and this time they were told that Edward had recently left the farm and (despite the fact that the Society should have been *in loco parentis* until he was twenty-one) they said they had no way of knowing where he was. A letter dated 25 September 1987 which the Society sent to another member of the family, who was independently searching for Edward, contradicted this: "Edward was at our farm school from 1953 until 1963 [when he was sixteen] and he remained in contact with us until 1970 [when he was twenty-three]. Since then we lost contact and have been unable to find any trace of him."

Efforts by his family to trace Edward failed until they made contact with the Child Migrants Trust. The Trust found Edward, still living in Australia, who thanked his family "for bothering to take the trouble to find me". He intends to visit Britain as soon as he can to see the family he did not even know existed.

Even when the Trust has traced relatives, the problems aren't always over. Supposing, for instance, the mother remarried thirty-five years ago, she has children from this marriage, and then she has the trauma of her previous child turning up with all the guilt and intense emotions involved. One mother, in Britain, who had seen a brief news programme about the appalling experiences of some of the child migrants in Australia, was approached by the Trust on behalf of her daughter, still living in Australia. "Oh, my God," said the mother. "She wasn't one of those children, was she?" The mother, who had placed her daughter for adoption with a Catholic society in Britain, had no idea her daughter had been sent to Australia.

This highlights the complications that exist when you try to reunite a family in these circumstances. How, for instance, does a parent cope with a son or daughter saying, "Well, for forty years I was told I was an orphan"? How do they say, "But they told me you were adopted, they told me you were in a family. I never knew you'd gone"? And how do they answer when they are asked, "But why didn't you ever try to find me?" They feel their child cannot want to know them and that they, in turn, cannot face them.

Broaching a matter that has been hidden for years is not easy. As Margaret Humphreys says:

> What do you do when you know you're going to see somebody who may not have told their husband or children? I have to assume that no one knows. How do they feel, how will they react? Can they cope with these issues at this stage in their life? But they know more than anybody about that loss. And I haven't yet had to tell any parent why I wish to see them. They have all told me. They know, more than anybody, the unfinished business in their life.

The apprehension and anxiety felt by the son or daughter is also very strong. They concentrate their hopes on finding one or both parents or a sister or brother so hard, that when they are told that they have been found, they have to face the fear of rejection. As one woman said:

> I'm worried about taking any steps to find my mother. She could be married now with a family who know nothing about me. Why give them trouble? If she does want to know me, then that's fine. But if she doesn't that's all right, because that's her life and this is mine. All my life I've been saying I don't care. Maybe that's something I say so I don't get hurt by it. Maybe deep down I do.

The Trust keeps those in Australia constantly informed about how progress is going. That way a picture is built up gradually and any decisions are made jointly. If the Trust is on the verge of finding a parent, the son or daughter is told. And even then, as Margaret Humphreys says:

> I write to say, "It looks as if this could be your mother." Although the documentation can tell me it is her, at the end of the day she could still say she isn't. If I find out that Bill Smith's mother had two daughters, I would write and say, "I've found these births, I think they may be, we can't be sure, but it looks like . . ." So it's no shock when I write and tell them the outcome.

There are several options once a parent is found. If a relation, perhaps an aunt, already knows the background, the child migrant is asked whether it would be advisable to ask for the aunt's help in approaching the mother. Or it may be that the Trust feels a visit is more appropriate than a letter or phone call: that someone needs to be with the parent, offering support. The Trust is aware of situations which have come to a tragic end because the child migrant has taken matters in his or her own hands and made the first contact.

Because the Trust tries to offer a sensitive and responsive service, it operates with anonymity in the first instance. If the decision is made to write to a mother, the Trust will write a letter on the lines of, "I am in touch with somebody you knew many years ago and I wonder if we could meet somewhere to discuss this." If such a letter is read by anyone else, it means nothing, but it is profoundly significant to a parent. The replies are almost invariably positive. The Trust is not expecting an emotional welcome – for a parent to say "I want to see my son, My Son, next week." There is so much for the parent to take in, as well as dealing with his or her own reactions. The outcome of the talk is then relayed to Australia. One woman, who was told her sister in Britain had been contacted, still couldn't believe it, even when her sister wrote to her:

> I opened the letter up and I looked at the address and I looked at the address again and I couldn't go past it! And by this time, my husband's looking over my shoulder and he's saying, "Read it, *read* it, oh my God!" I was literally a balloon about to burst, everything just *poured* out. And I rang her, my sister, the next day in England, I had to ring her, I couldn't wait to write. I was so scared. I started crying and I said, "It's your sister Pat from Australia." And she said, "My God, my God!" And she started crying and we didn't know what to say. And I said, "I'm here, I'll write to you. I got your letter, it was wonderful." Oh, it was a moment and a half. And all that day I kept crying.

It's an emotional time and skilled professional help is essential. The Child Migrants Trust cannot both research the families in Britain and be with the son or daughter in Australia at the crucial time. What is needed is funding for professionally-trained helpers in Australia who would be able to offer the support needed throughout the delicate and sensitive period of research, while similarly trained workers in Britain offer counselling and support to the entire family.

The comfort of a personal visit is important. Being told news of a family, or child, abruptly, without any counselling, can be too much of a shock. People need to be able to express their fears and anxieties. Sylvia Randall became very anxious in Australia while waiting for the news about her family. She originally wrote to the Trust to give them the little information she had about herself. She had never been able to believe that she had no relatives at all.

Ever since I was a teenager, I had been asking the Catholic Welfare people in Australia about my parents. They couldn't tell us anything – or did not want to tell us anything. The priest told me that my mother was in Holloway prison.

She was shocked to find that her birth certificate, which she had obtained herself from Somerset House, gave her a different surname. Writing to the Catholic Home in England that had sent her out, Sylvia was told that her mother had visited her at the Home in 1943. As she had collected her two other children that same year from different Homes, she might well have been trying to reclaim her third child, Sylvia.

The Trust researched Sylvia's family. "I spent the day she [Margaret Humphreys] was going to arrive [in Australia] curled up in a little ball on my bed. If she hadn't turned up when she did, I think I would be in a mental hospital again. The strain was terrible."

Margaret told her that she had a half-brother and sister. Sylvia was overjoyed, but also worried:

I asked her if they would like me. Margaret went back to England and contacted them and then rang to say my half-sister was going to telephone me. At first, I did not really believe it, but when she did and I asked her questions – I knew she was part of me. My husband gave his job up to get early superannuation so I could go to England. More than anything else he wants my *peace of mind*.

The Catholics are still lying to us. My husband once rang Monsignor Crennan in Sydney [director of the Australian Federal Catholic Immigration Committee, whose involvement with child migration dates back to 1949] for any information on me and he wrote back and said we knew all there was to know, there was nothing else to tell us. He flew over to England and came back and rang my husband to tell him that the Child Migrants Trust would never be able to tell us anything. And here I am sitting in my sister's house in England, all through the Trust.

Monsignor Crennan has gone on record as saying, "I don't feel any responsibility for them [child migrants] at all." He justifies this by saying, "We didn't arrange for them to come. We were nominated by the Children's Department to find places for them."

The agencies involved with the child migration scheme failed to recognise the long-term implications. Some agencies are still denying these. Barnardo's, in Australia, is one that recognises its responsibility to the British children sent out and has appointed an After Care Co-ordinator to provide them with support, information and counselling. Any child migrant contacting Barnardo's is told of its "Open File" policy – in operation now for some ten years – and what kind of material is held on file. If any ex-Barnardo child wants to see it, the Co-ordinator helps to prepare him or her for any judgements it might contain. It's a necessary precaution; many child migrants have been sent their files by their agencies or have finally discovered them and have been understandably upset to find comments on themselves or their parents. One woman was particularly angry to find her mother dubbed "of dubious repute" – with no evidence to support this.

Barnardo's in Australia makes the point that Australian children placed in the same orphanages as the British child migrants had an equally harsh time. But at least they had some hope of remaining in contact with their family, or of tracing them without these tremendous difficulties.

When the child migrants do find some sort of file on themselves, they at last discover a past, a certain sense of identity. But they still have the long and laborious task of finding their family. The need is heartfelt. When Margaret Humphreys and David Spicer, barrister and trustee of the Child Migrants Trust, made a second visit to Australia, they received a warm welcome from those who felt their needs were at last being recognised. The response was phenomenal and they returned with over 200 requests for help. Some people travelled up to four hours to make sure they saw them before they returned to England. The pleas to find their families were desperate.

The increasing demands on the services of the Child Migrants Trust clearly shows the value of a professional, specialised agency which is both independent and international in its work. An organisation which is not associated with any of the earlier policies and practices of child migration schemes, is well placed to offer a service to former child migrants and members of their families. Some of these would be most reluctant to seek help from the agencies originally involved in their emigration, while other agencies have closed down completely. The surviving agencies should now recognise the need for this *neutral* service. Can they not now work with the Trust to help heal some of the scars of separation, now that the need is so apparent? As one of the child migrants said, "We still can't believe it. We still can't believe that anybody cares. *Anybody.*"

12

Post-mortem

What is so extraordinary about the child migration scheme is that at no time were any legal safeguards made governing the welfare of the many thousands of child migrants sent out by the voluntary societies. Under the Children Act, 1948, the Secretary of State was given the legal power to control the emigration arrangements made by the voluntary organisations but this was never used. No agency was required to register. The last group of children was sent out to Australia in 1967 but it was not until *January 1982* that any regulations were made – well over a decade too late.

From a historical perspective, the treatment of children over the years has left much to be desired, but it is shaming to realise that some of the worst treatment of child migrants took place after the Second World War. Did no one care? In fact, many did, but their belief that the government intended to bring in legislation curbing the voluntary societies proved their undoing.

The first promising move after the war, when the attitude to children in need of care became more sympathetic, came when the government set up a Committee of Enquiry, chaired by Myra Curtis, CBE, "To enquire into existing methods of providing for children who from loss of parents or from any other cause whatever are deprived of a normal home life with their parents or relatives; and to consider what further measures should be taken to ensure that these children are brought up under conditions best calculated to compensate them for the lack of parental care." It concluded that, "Children separated from ordinary parental care lacked affection and interest and also felt the loss of stability."

The Curtis Committee took evidence from voluntary organisations involved in child migration schemes and was concerned that, "this opportunity is given only to children of fine physique and good mental equipment. These are precisely the children for whom satisfactory openings could be found in this Country and in present day conditions this particular method of providing for the deprived child is not one that we especially wish to see extended." It decided that children who *wished* to emigrate should be allowed to do so, but warned, "We should however strongly deprecate their setting out in life under less thorough care and supervision than they would have at home."

The Curtis report was presented to Parliament in September 1946, and formed the basis of the most far-reaching legislation ever made regarding deprived children: the Children Act of 1948. This effectively placed the whole ministerial responsibility for the care of deprived children with the Home Secretary.

One organisation, The British Federation of Social Workers, was anxious to influence the Children Bill's provisions on child migration, particularly over selection procedures. It found, for example, that some children recruited by the London Council of the Fairbridge Society to go to Southern Rhodesia were not "deprived", but living with both parents. The specialist panel set up to investigate sent representatives to the children's homes and often "found a completely different picture from that which had been presented in the first Report". In 1946, the Federation was blithely reassured by the Fairbridge Farm Schools of Australia and Canada, "That there would not be any large-scale migration of children" (there already was), but they found that no arrangements were ever made for foster homes in Canada or Australia and that all records, apart from medical information, remained at Fairbridge's London headquarters. The Federation disliked the enforced censorship of letters to or from the children, who were not encouraged to keep up with relations in England; and found legal responsibilities were vague and not clearly understood.

While the Bill was being debated, child migrants were leaving in their hundreds for farm schools and orphanages in Australia. MPs criticised the large, impersonal institutions but their views did not affect what was actually happening.

The Children Bill contained two clauses on child migration. Clause 17 dealt with children in local authority care: these would only be allowed to emigrate with the Secretary of State's consent, and if it benefited them. Clause 32 concerned children cared for by voluntary organisations. This said the Secretary of State "may by regulations" control emigration arrangements. There was immediately pressure to change the word *may* to *shall*. Speaking in the House of Lords on 13 April 1948, Lord Llewellyn said:

It would be a great satisfaction to the Societies who do this work best if they knew that some of the bodies who do not do it so well could be brought up to the mark, so that children are not sent out without any regard to whether they are likely to go to decent homes when they get overseas, whether they are themselves in a fit condition and are the kind of children who ought to be sent abroad.

The Lord Chancellor, Viscount Jowitt's reply, was crucial and because of its reassurances, the British Federation of Social Workers withdrew its insistence on amendments to Clause 32:

My Lords ... I can give an assurance that the Home Office intend to secure that children should not be emigrated unless there is absolute satisfaction that proper arrangements have been made for the care and upbringing of each child.

A few still regarded the Bill as inadequate. For example, Mr Wilson Harris, MP for Cambridge University and editor of the *Spectator,* said:

To send a child of fourteen to sixteen away from these shores to some distant country, whether in the Dominions or outside, is to submit that child to what is sometimes a rather alarming experience. It is, therefore, of the utmost importance that the fullest attention should be given both to the selection of the children at this end and to their reception at the other.

Mr Harris might have been even more worried had he realised the speed at which agencies were accelerating the rate of child migration, and that the children involved were more likely to be as young as five. In reply to all the doubts raised, the Home Secretary announced, "All the points which have been raised by my Honourable friends are those which will have to be covered by the regulations when they are made ... In drafting the first regulations, I shall see that adequate attention is given to them ... The regulations will certainly require adequate arrangements to be made for ensuring that the child who is being emigrated has the same after-care as that which is required for the Local Authority child."

These assurances satisfied MPs and the Bill became law. Section 33 (Clause 32 in the Bill) gave the Secretary of State the power to make regulations that would control the way the voluntary organisations arranged child migration.

In 1953, the government established the Overseas Migration Board which enthusiastically supported child migration schemes. It encouraged the Home Office, for example, to consider the best way of bringing the facilities available for child migrants to the attention of local authorities, in order to boost migration figures still higher. It also suggested to the government that it raise its weekly maintenance payments to £1 a week per child. In 1955–6, maintenance allowances for each child migrant, paid until he or she reached sixteen, had come to a peak at £36,396. Substantial sums were also paid for passage costs.

In 1958, the Migration Board set out details on the various agencies connected with child migration and their operations. Those still involved were: the Catholic Child Welfare Council; the Church of England Council for Commonwealth and Empire Settlement; the Church of Scotland Committee on Social Service; the Northcote Children's Emigration Fund for Australia; Dr Barnardo's; the Big Brother Movement; the Fairbridge Society; the National Children's Home; and the Salvation Army. But despite the fact that large-scale child migration was continuing, it was no longer a public issue. The next legislation which affected it came within the Child Care Act 1980 and the part of the 1948 Act which gave the Secretary of State the power to make regulations regarding the welfare of child migrants sent out by voluntary societies, turned up as Section 62. When the Act went into print a note was added, "At the time of going to press, no regulations had been made under this section." Only in January *1982* did it become a legal requirement for any voluntary association to get the consent of the Secretary of State before sending a child abroad.

The misjudgements of the child migration scheme destroyed the lives of thousands of children and cannot be spelt out too often, to stop the same mistakes from ever being made again. For as one MP who admitted that her children might have been materially better off in a Home abroad, said:

> No one would have dared to come to me and say that, because of that fact, they thought that there was a far better place for my children – Australia. It is true that we can benefit the child materially, but we might break their hearts and that is something they must always consider.

Child migration was meant to be in the best interests of the child. But throughout its history, the children never came first. "Coming out to Australia," said a child migrant, "was like coming from the warmth to the cold. I'll never forget. *Why* did they do it?"

FURTHER INFORMATION

If you would like further information about the Child Migrants Trust, or would like to give a donation, please write to:

**The Child Migrants Trust
8 Kingston Road
West Bridgford
Nottingham NG2 7AQ**

BIBLIOGRAPHY

Bagnell, Kenneth, *The Little Immigrants* (Macmillan of Canada 1980)

Barnardo, Mrs and Marchant, James, *Memoirs of the late Dr Barnardo* (Hodder & Stoughton 1907)

Corbett, Gail H., *Barnardo Children in Canada* (Woodland Publishing, Canada 1981)

Edmondson, William, *Making Rough Places Plain: fifty years' work of the Manchester and Salford Boys' and Girls' Refuges* (Sherratt & Hughes 1921)

Autobiography of Kingsley Fairbridge (OUP 1927)

Fairbridge, Ruby, *Fairbridge Farm: the building of a farm school* (Paterson Press, Perth 1948)

Harrison, Phyllis (Ed.), *The Home Children* (Watson & Dwyer Publishing Ltd, Winnipeg, Manitoba 1979)

Huxley, Elspeth, *Atlantic Ordeal: the story of Mary Cornish* (Chatto & Windus 1941)

Jackson, C., *Who Will Take Our Children* (Methuen 1985)

Johnson, Stanley C., *A History of Emigration* (Routledge & Sons 1913)

Macpherson, Annie, *The Little Matchbox Makers*

Magnusson, Ann, *The Village: a history of Quarrier's* (Quarrier's Homes 1984)

Marriott, John A. R., *Empire Settlement* (OUP 1927)

Middleton, N., *When Family Failed* (Gollancz 1971)

Parr, Joy, *Labouring Children* (Croom Helm 1980)

Rose, J., *For the Sake of the Children* (Hodder & Stoughton 1987)

Sutherland, N., *Children in English-Canadian Society* (Toronto University Press 1976)

Wagner, Gillian, *Children of the Empire* (Weidenfeld & Nicholson 1982)

Reports and Papers

Child Migrations to Australia (HMSO Cmd 9832 August 1956)

Departmental Committee on Agricultural Settlement in the British Colonies (HMSO Vol 1 Col 2978 HMSO 1906)

Kelso, J. J., *A Special Report on the Immigration of British Children* (Canada 1897)

Moss, J., *Child Migration to Australia* (Report to Home Office 1953)

Report by Andrew Doyle to the President of the Local Government Board on Emigration of Pauper Children to Canada (Parliamentary Papers 1875)

Report of the British Overseas Settlement Delegation to Canada 1924 (Parliamentary Papers 1924)

Report of the Care of Children Committee (HMSO Cmd 6922 1946)

Report on the Proceedings of the Committee of the House of Commons on Immigration and Colonisation (Canada 1875)

Index

600